LIVING WITH LOCOS

LIVING WITH LOCOS

Charlie Meacher

BRADFORD BARTON

ISBN 0 85153 392 2

printed by CTP Ltd for the publishers
D. BRADFORD BARTON LIMITED
Trethellan House Truro Cornwall

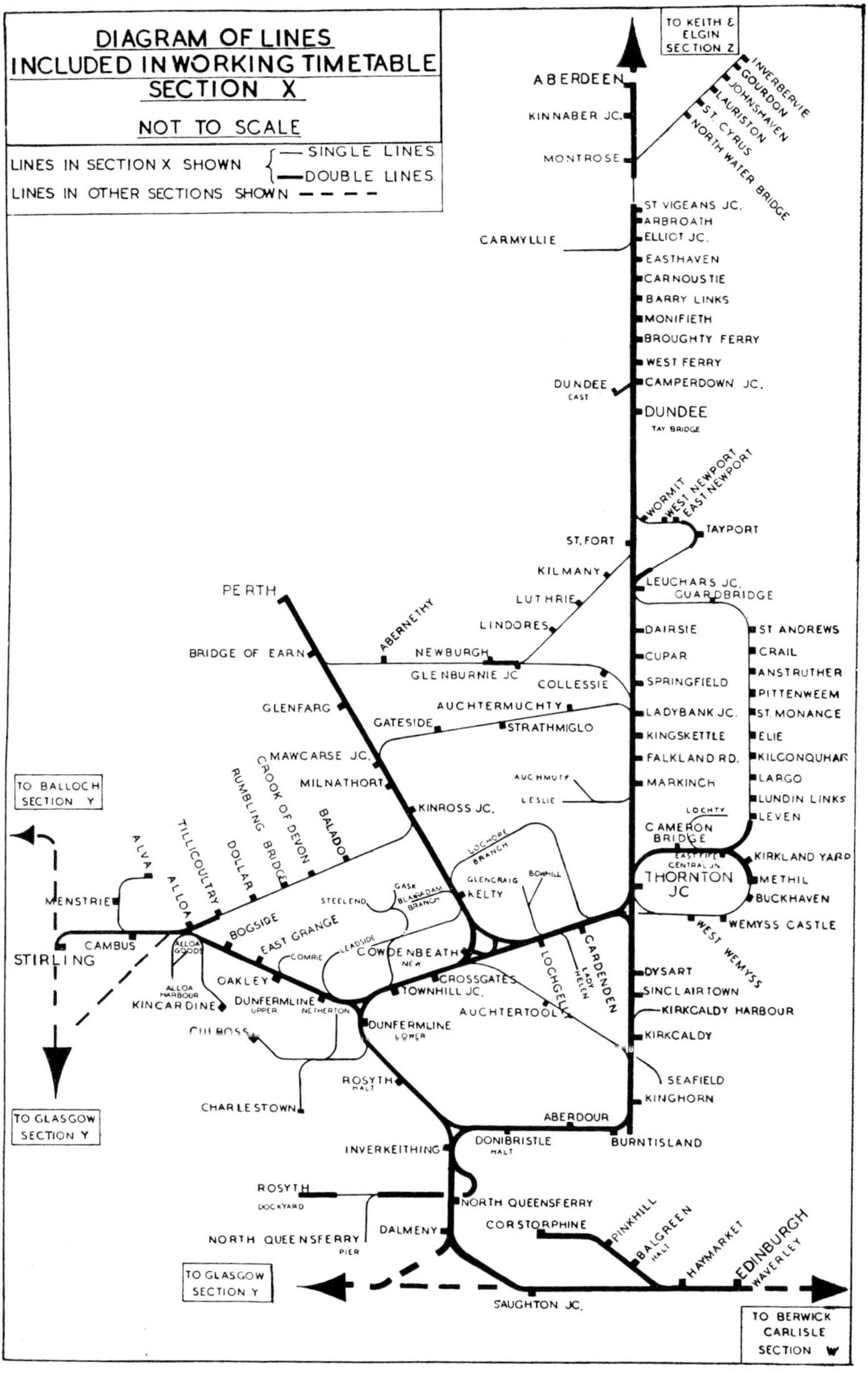
DIAGRAM OF LINES
INCLUDED IN WORKING TIMETABLE
SECTION X
NOT TO SCALE
LINES IN SECTION X SHOWN — SINGLE LINES
— DOUBLE LINES
LINES IN OTHER SECTIONS SHOWN - - - -
TO KEITH & ELGIN SECTION Z
ABERDEEN
KINNABER JC.
MONTROSE
INVERBERVIE
GOURDON
JOHNSHAVEN
LAURISTON
ST. CYRUS
NORTH WATER BRIDGE
ST VIGEANS JC.
ARBROATH
ELLIOT JC.
CARMYLLIE
EASTHAVEN
CARNOUSTIE
BARRY LINKS
MONIFIETH
BROUGHTY FERRY
WEST FERRY
CAMPERDOWN JC.
DUNDEE EAST
DUNDEE TAY BRIDGE
WORMIT
WEST NEWPORT
EAST NEWPORT
TAYPORT
ST. FORT
KILMANY
LEUCHARS JC.
GUARDBRIDGE
LUTHRIE
LINDORES
PERTH
ABERNETHY
NEWBURGH
BRIDGE OF EARN
GLENBURNIE JC
COLLESSIE
DAIRSIE
CUPAR
SPRINGFIELD
ST ANDREWS
CRAIL
ANSTRUTHER
PITTENWEEM
ST. MONANCE
ELIE
KILCONQUHAR
LARGO
LUNDIN LINKS
LEVEN
GLENFARG
AUCHTERMUCHTY
GATESIDE
STRATHMIGLO
LADYBANK JC.
KINGSKETTLE
FALKLAND RD.
MAWCARSE JC.
MILNATHORT
AUCHMUTY
LESLIE
MARKINCH
KINROSS JC.
LOCHTY
CAMERON BRIDGE
TO BALLOCH SECTION Y
ALVA
TILLICOULTRY
DOLLAR
RUMBLING BRIDGE
CROOK OF DEVON
BALADO
LOCHORE BRANCH
EAST FIFE CENTRAL JN.
THORNTON JC
KIRKLAND YARD
METHIL
BUCKHAVEN
MENSTRIE
ALLOA
GASK
BLAIRADAM BRANCH
STEELEND
GLENCRAIG
BOWHILL
KELTY
WEMYSS CASTLE
WEST WEMYSS
CAMBUS
STIRLING
ALLOA GOODS
BOGSIDE
EAST GRANGE
COMRIE
LEADSIDE
COWDENBEATH NEW
LOCHGELLY
LADY HELEN
CARDENDEN
OAKLEY
CROSSGATES
TOWNHILL JC.
DYSART
SINCLAIRTOWN
ALLOA HARBOUR
KINCARDINE
DUNFERMLINE UPPER
NETHERTON
AUCHTERTOOL
KIRKCALDY HARBOUR
DUNFERMLINE LOWER
KIRKCALDY
SEAFIELD
ROSYTH HALT
KINGHORN
CHARLESTOWN
ABERDOUR
TO GLASGOW SECTION Y
INVERKEITHING
DONIBRISTLE HALT
BURNTISLAND
ROSYTH DOCKYARD
NORTH QUEENSFERRY
NORTH QUEENSFERRY PIER
DALMENY
CORSTORPHINE
PINKHILL
BALGREEN HALT
HAYMARKET
EDINBURGH WAVERLEY
TO GLASGOW SECTION Y
SAUGHTON JC.
TO BERWICK CARLISLE SECTION W

PREFACE

This sequel to *L.N.E.R. Footplate Memories* is by request from the many people who enjoy reading about steam engines and enginemen. The subject matter needs no introduction, for famous trains like The Flying Scotsman have ensured that Edinburgh's railways are well enough known. But, since part of this book centres on Fife I feel that 'The Kingdom', as it is popularly called, is worthy of introduction because of its distinctive railway history. This peninsula on the east coast of Scotland lies between the Firths of Forth and Tay and possesses two famous rail bridges. In either direction through Fife, apart from short stretches, a train's level running begins and ends on these bridges. The place may be fit for a king but it does not favour railways. The terrain is not at all suited to the iron road and in the extreme Fife has the steepest railway gradient on British Railways, namely, the 1 in 20 on the Kirkcaldy Harbour branch. This line was worked by Class J88 engines and on more than a few occasions one has had to be fished out of the drink as a result of a runaway. The crane doing the fishing was worked to and from the harbour by three J88s while a big engine waited to take over on the main line; No.68341 was the last Pug to take a dive, in January 1955, and was the first of her class to be scrapped after the escapade.

The modern County of Fife has an area of 505 square miles and is the sixteenth in size of Scottish counties. The greatest length of the county, from Fifeness to Kennetpans, is 41 miles, and its breadth, from Burntisland to Newburgh, is 21 miles. The coastline of the county is about 115 miles long.

Mobility, for the great majority of the people had, of course, to await the arrival of mechanical transport. Mineral railways with horse-drawn wagons were laid down in several parts of Fife during the eighteenth century to facilitate the movement of coal to the harbours, one of the most notable being the line from Fordell to the tiny port of St. Davids. But the present system, unlike that of many other areas, does not derive directly therefrom. The lay-out existing today had its origins in the long persisting dream of an all-East Coast route from London to Aberdeen. The ferries at Burntisland and Tayport naturally claimed attention, and the first main lines resulted in the linking of these places, in two stages. The first was the completion of a line from Burntisland to Cupar, with a line branching off to Newburgh at Ladybank, this being later carried on to Perth, still the most obvious gateway to the country north of the Tay. These portions of line were opened for traffic during 1847. The line from Cupar to Tayport is understood to have been opened in the following year but, though this extension was constructed under the terms of a separate Act, the project was undoubtedly conceived as a whole. Only one of the county's four most populous areas is touched by the main line and, though this would not matter greatly if it were possible for them to be fed on conveniently, such has not been the case. Dunfermline and Leven have been connected along the valley of the Ore to Thornton, rather than over the shorter distance to Burntisland in the first case and along the coast to Kirkcaldy in the second. In the east, St. Andrews stood too far apart and on the wrong side of the River Eden, so the link there had to be placed further north. Technical and physical considerations dictated the original choice of Thornton, Leuchars and Ladybank but a glance at a road map makes it clear how much more conveniently the railway could have served internal needs had it been possible to substitute Kirkcaldy, St. Andrews and Cupar. One result is that Dunfermline has been badly cut off from much of the rest of the county. The coming of buses accentuated this unsuitability while, at Thornton, subsidence has been a serious worry. The opening of the great bridges over the Tay and Forth, in 1878 and 1890, greatly enhanced the quickness and comfort of main line travel but increased the pull of Dundee and Edinburgh as centres for shopping, work or education. Dunfermline in particular was brought much nearer to Edinburgh.

Mention may be made of one oddity, slight in itself, but perhaps symbolic of how early days have continued to dominate Fife's railways. Kirkcaldy Town Council, in return for their support of the Forth Bridge project, exacted the promise from the railways that the fare to Edinburgh should not be increased. It stood at one shilling for many a day, when the shorter journey from Dunfermline to Edinburgh cost much more and time has seen the gap widen as proportionate increases have gone on fares.

Being a small county, Fife was in danger of losing its identity under the Local Government (Scotland) Act, 1973. Fifers fought this all the way and when the new authorities were established on 16 May 1975, Fife survived geographically as the smallest of 9 regions, although populationwise the Fife Region is in the middle of the league. But, like so many other places, Fife could not parry the Beeching axe and its railways were drastically trimmed. Nevertheless, the main arteries survive and the two great rail bridges spanning the Forth and Tay estuaries are vital links joining Fife with the national rail network.

The main line railway through Fife is one of the most difficult stretches of railway in all Britain and a severe handicap to fast running on the East Coast. The high speed running from London to the North is suddenly curtailed as soon as the train moves on to the Forth Bridge at 40m.p.h. North of the Bridge there is a two mile descent of 1 in 70 to Inverkeithing with a restriction of 25m.p.h. through the station and junction. Southbound trains have to cope with this restriction before tackling the long climb to the Bridge through Inverkeithing (420 yards) and North Queensferry (460 yards) tunnels.

Heading north beyond Inverkeithing there is a climb of 2¼ miles to Dalgetty summit at 1 in 94 and from there a drop, mostly at 1 in 100 past Aberdour, to 1½ miles short of Burntisland.

Curvature prevents any advantage being taken of these gradients and the next ascent cannot be rushed because of the 20m.p.h. speed restriction round Burntisland curve. Southbound trains starting from here do so for a short distance at 1 in 77; continuing north there is a climb of 1 in 305–128 to Kinghorn tunnel (265 yards) through which speed is restricted to 30m.p.h. Local lore has it that the bend in Kinghorn tunnel was brought about when the foremen working on its construction disagreed and deliberately went off course while boring through from opposite ends.

From Kinghorn there is a level stretch, until half a mile short of Kirkcaldy climbing is resumed finally for two miles at 1 in 100–114 to 28½ milepost. From here two miles down at 1 in 130–170 (ending with a brief 1 in 67) lead to Thornton where mining subsidence used to enforce a speed restriction of 30 but this has been lifted since mining operations ceased and Thornton Junction station was demolished. The only speed restriction here now is through the junction to and from Thornton West (15m.p.h.) and through the junction to the Methil line (10m.p.h.).

After Thornton, climbing soon begins again, first for a mile at 1 in 129, then, after a short level, at 1 in 102 for 1½ miles to Lochmuir summit. North of Lochmuir, Falkland Road bank faces southbound trains, 3½ miles at 1 in 95–111 starting just south of Ladybank. Between Dalmeny and Falkland Road there is a ceiling on all maximum speeds of 60m.p.h. but apart from the moderate slowings through Ladybank (40m.p.h.) Cupar (55m.p.h.) and Leuchars (55m.p.h.). 70 is permitted from there to the Tay Bridge.

Beyond Dundee there is scope for higher speeds but Fife remains a real thorn in the side of time-table planners and the new high speed image of British Rail. It is no different between Inverkeithing Central Junction and Thornton Junction via Cowdenbeath where there is a maximum speed of 65m.p.h. reducing at Cowdenbeath to 60 – indeed, there are as many speed restrictions as mileposts. Further north on the single line between Ladybank Junction and Hilton Junction (Perth) via Newburgh the maximum permissible speed is 45m.p.h.

It will be appreciated, therefore, that the railways in Fife do not easily lend themselves to record-breaking runs. Nevertheless, the railwaymen, like their kind elsewhere, were the same dedicated breed who applied themselves wholly to the job. They say, "It takes a long spoon to sup wi' a Fifer," but I like to think my spoon was sufficiently long enough to become accepted during my time at Thornton.

CHAPTER I

The contrast between diesel and steam – St. Margarets depot at Edinburgh – Joe McCann and a Glen – a big shunt and a disabled K3 – Pacifics tender-first – foiling a train robbery – coaling at St. Margarets – run-down V2s – characterful drivers – a runaway J38 – an accident to a Clan

IN PRESENT TIMES almost everything about locomotive driving is uninteresting and even wearisome to the average driver; to his assistant sitting idly in the cab for long hours it seems close to purgatory. These men know beforehand the type of locomotive or rail car they will be sitting in and that just about sums up their total effort. One might say in effect they are confined to a mobile prison on fixed rails with minimum physical demand. Admittedly, a driver is expected to be mentally alert to his job but such is the boredom of modern rail traction that concentration can all too easily be lost, with dire consequences such as a signal passed at danger or, worse still, a collision. With the steam engine such accidents happened for different reasons, least of all boredom.

In contrast to the 'on tap' power of today's locomotive, the steam engine lent itself to the creation of power by the sheer physical effort of the fireman and very often the driver, too. These men knew the demands that awaited them as soon as they took duty. They were mentally tuned to and fully aware of what was expected. This was a constant challenge to a man's ability and such is his vanity that he seldom failed to rise to the occasion. If it was not pride in achievement that he felt it might well be the shame of the failure that he feared. Whatever it was, the challenge was seldom avoided.

Just as St. Margarets shed was a constant operating challenge to generations of supervisors so, too, were the numerous classes of engines to the footplatemen. Without fire, these engines soon became rusting hulks exposed as they were to the elements. Engines in steam were grimey things and positively filthy after standing for a period in the soot-laden environment of 64A. A visit to the place was sufficient to justify a hot bath whilst to grip handrails and climb into a cab resulted in oily, dirt-ingrained hands and the need for strong solvent to remove this grime. There were no magic cleansers in my steam days and to get our hands reasonably clean we used soft soap and a lot of hard rubbing on the worn brickwork near the bothy sink. More often than not our black faces and red-rimmed eyes remained so until we reached home and more civilised ablution.

All these apparent discomforts were accepted as part of the job and, although we changed our overalls every week, our caps and serge jackets, suitably coloured to disguise the dirt, were worn for a year or more depending on the availability of new issues and the individual engineman. One had only to look at a Rule Book kept in an open breast pocket to realise the amount of dirt the jacket harboured. The exposed edge of the book was a sharp contrast of black to the hidden white pages. But in steam days air pollution and personal discomfort were accepted as normal and it is only now that comparisons can be made.

The clinical sobriety of a modern traction depot never fails to impress me when I recall the intense activity and excited feelings that abounded in the vulcan environments of St. Margarets. Men are undoubtedly influenced by their surroundings plus the nature of their work and this was obvious to the most casual observer. Motive power working conditions today do not bring out the locomotiveman's distinctive personal character so well as when he was in association with the temperamental steam engine.

I was close at hand when top link driver Joe McCann signed on duty one day. After exchanging a few pleasantries with the time-keeper he moved along to the running office window and stuck his head through a low aperture designed for communicating with the supervisor or his assistant. "What's on the job today?" asked Joe. Jimmy Brown, the running foreman, eyed the wee driver over his glasses and mumbled a greeting. Looking down at the engine sheet, the foreman was slow to find the particular engine number but Joe read it upside down and uttered in disgust "2484 – a Glen!" "That's a good engine," said

Broonie in a salesmanlike manner. Joe ignored him and, turning away from the smiling gaffer to where I stood, he murmured, "That silly b—— doesn't know an engine from a wagon . . ."

Joe and I went over to the running shed together; as we crossed the main line the shunt signal was pulled off and a Green Arrow passed in front of us hauling 2484 *Glen Lyon*. Joe's eyes followed the movement on its way to the tunnel then, suddenly realising what was happening, he bellowed out to no one in particular, "Hey! – where are you going with my engine?" Just then the shed foreman appeared and informed Joe that his engine was a failure and on its way to the Crane Road to await repairs. "You're getting 2487 now," said the foreman. "I'll get somebody to give you a hand to make it ready." "Give me a hand!" exclaimed Joe. "I'm no making any bloody engines ready – I threw away my greasing kit years ago!"

There were usually spare men to help out in these situations and regular greasers, too, would lend a hand, but such rapid preparation didn't appease Joe, not even when the running foreman joined in and helped to fill the tank. Joe was well known for his tantrums and could usually be heard before he was seen but he was left speechless that day when, amidst all the intense activity round his engine, there arrived a fitter's mate with a barrow load of brake blocks which he unloaded at Joe's feet. "Don't tell me this thing's to block," said Joe disbelievingly, but the blocker nodded in the affirmative. "Oh, tae hell!" said Joe, "I'm going home!" and he wandered off in the direction of the bothy, there to cool down while *Glen Arklet* was reblocked.

This is only an instance of what made up the daily (and nightly) round in St. Margarets. This is what kept the adrenalin flowing and increased the blood pressure. Engines in various stages of preparation or repair stood around while others moved through disposal, all seemingly competing in atmospheric pollution. *Glen Arklet* outdid them all, while men raced against time to get her ready for the road. As oil poured into the motions and brake blocks were slung into position, the loud purring of primary air through the firebars sent shock waves to the ear drums. Soon the foreman was on the phone telling the signalman 2487 was ready for the Waverley to work the 3.45p.m. Berwick Slow; then the hurriedly prepared engine moved tender-first to the signal where Joe climbed aboard to join his fireman.

Not long after Joe disappeared through the tunnel I was roped in to assist with a big shunt. This entailed coupling eight engines together – some in steam, others dead – and moving them clear of a K3 ready off repairs at the buffer stop. The exercise called for team effort and when the engines were manned and ready to move under the direct supervision of the running foreman this worthy advised the signalman what was required.

St. Margarets signalmen were wary of big shunts which often caused delay to main line trains but, after being assured there were plenty of men and power to make it a quick move, the signalman pulled off the shunt signal. Drivers had already taken the strain and couplings were tight, those who couldn't see the signal being alerted by the foreman's whistle and shouts. As the steam regulators were opened simultaneously, the wheels danced and tractive effort was lost. It seemed a row of volcanoes had erupted as smoke and steam blasted from the chimneys, then the long crocodile began to move as the wheels slowly revolved on sanded rails.

The procession was well through the tunnel and blocking the down main line before the last engine was clear to release the K3 into another road. Charlie Bonnyman was on the Gresley Mogul and to me, on the rear engine of the shunt, it seemed he was never going to come out. Impatiently I hurried down the shed to see what the trouble was and as I approached the K3 there was a loud bang and the right connecting rod bent in the middle. Water gushed from the cylinder cocks and, in wonderment, Charlie B. emerged from the cab.

The loud bang had attracted Jim Walinck, the mechanical foreman, and as he surveyed the damage, water still poured from the cylinder cocks, gallons of it. Jim wasn't very pleased and quietly cursed drivers in general. "Alright," he said, "the engines stopped – no more fire." This he chalked on the tender for the benefit of the steamraiser. Meanwhile, the running foreman was coming hastily down the shed to investigate the delay while the signalman paced his domain as main line trains formed a queue at Piershill and Craigentinny. The big shunt was eventually waved back into the road it had vacated and the K3 stayed put for further repairs – all because the cylinder cocks had been closed over a long period, allowing water to collect and prove an immovable hydraulic force against the pistons. Something had to give and in this case it had been the connecting rod; it might well have been the cylinder cover or side rods.

In order to make a shunt of this magnitude, four locomotives were brought to full working pressure. This meant the fires were spread about the box and liberal quantities of coal shovelled on. There was no time for normal steam-raising to develop and on these occasions combustion was encouraged by use of the poker, the hastened result being 'poker steam'. When the engines were again stabled there were fierce fires and much of the coal in the fireboxes unburnt. So, for long afterwards there was an incessant blowing-off of steam with the accompanying noise and a quick loss of water in the boiler. If the steam raiser wasn't fully attentive there was danger of a fusible plug rupturing and damage to the fire-box, too. There was incalculable waste of this nature over the years and the archaic loco depot in the east end of Edinburgh must have been continually in the red so far as the financial accountant was concerned.

The decision to shunt out the K3 would not be taken lightly. Successive shifts would ignore this engine off repairs while the tender emptied and the firebox filled up. Usually it was an acute shortage of power which prompted a supervisor to evacuate the shed and 'dig out' an engine at the buffer stop. He knew the disruption such a move would cause and there was no guarantee the repaired engine would be fit for traffic; in fact, there was a real risk that further defects would come to light as the engine moved under its own steam. It would require coal and the fire cleaned and gallons of oil for the motions and mechanical lubricators, to say nothing of cleaning the soot-encrusted cab and boiler. The best way to deal with the latter was an assault by a high-pressure hot water hose which cleared the mess in record time and kept down the dust.

After a major repair, an engine was usually 'run in' first on slow local trains before venturing farther afield on faster trains. This was especially necessary when axle boxes and big ends had been remetalled and was often the reason why big tender engines took the place of smaller types on slow goods or passenger trains. From the driver's point of view, they were quite unsuited for the job and one had only to run a short distance tender-first with these giants to appreciate how inconvenient they were. Provided the coal had been trimmed there was limited viewing from inside the cab of a K3 or V2, with only the sight of sky or high buildings. Raised semaphore signals could also be seen when stationary below same. But nothing could be seen from the inside of the cab of an A4 travelling tender-first and the rubber apron between cab roof and tender top combined with the apron plate on the floor to form a single enclosed space. In these conditions a driver had to climb half way through the window to observe signals round the side of the massive tender. This was no great inconvenience over short distances and with a light engine but the 5.19p.m. Brakes from Leith Walk was worked like this over a long distance.

Invariably there was an A4 on this important train, loaded with whisky and tobacco and other excisable goods under seal destined for the South. The engine originated from Gateshead and was one of the few diagrammed locomotives in St. Margarets; in fact, I cannot recall any high capacity engine at that depot consistently working the job for which it was diagrammed. The 5.19p.m. engine came into the coal store in the early morning and after disposal would remain on shed until afternoon. It left the depot about 4.38p.m. and went tender-first the short distance to Piershill Junction where it was stopped, then crossed to the branch line leading to Lochend Junction and Easter Road for Leith Walk, travelling chimney leading in that direction.

Prior to arrival at Leith Walk, the train had been vacuum-tested by the pilot engine and it only remained for the big Pacific to couple on and get under way. This is when the driver became a contortionist and depended more than ever on his mate for signal sighting. To me it always seemed ungainly for a high speed Pacific to be hauling a train tender-first and this was over a distance of about three miles to Niddrie West, where the Leith Walk traffic combined with other traffic for the final fling along the East Coast.

After negotiating a severe dip, known as 'the Hole', between Leith Walk and Lochend Junction, the line was on a slightly falling gradient to Portobello. This gave the fireman a chance to get his fire made up for the assault on the now defunct Lothian Lines, a single track which climbed high over the main line between Portobello East and Joppa. It was operated under the Lock and Block type of signalling, the built-in safety of which could cause delay to trains, but the '5.19 No.1 Brakes' could expect some priority and was given a running start at the hill. Not that the powerful Pacific was handicapped in any way; on the contrary it went backwards up that incline with power to spare.

At Niddrie North signalbox, high above the Carlisle main line (Waverley Route) there were three divisions on the Lothian Lines – to Wanton Walls and the East Coast, Niddrie South and the Carlisle via Hawick line, and Niddrie West which dealt with traffic from all parts of the compass – a very busy marshalling area with yards on either side of the Edinburgh suburban line. The '5.19' took the single line diverging to Niddrie West which was practically within sight of Niddrie North but for the curvature of the track and an intervening overhead bridge. A train on this part of the line was not readily seen and usually steam and smoke from the locomotive would draw attention to its presence, although the signalbox instruments and interlocking kept the signalman alert to the occupancy of the line. It was on this 'camouflaged' section I stood with the '5.19' one evening as light was fading, waiting to be signalled into Niddrie West yard.

After twisting and stretching out to see signals it was a relief to sit comfortably in the driver's seat with feet up on the reverser looking along the boiler and snake-like train. Although on a curve I could see the guard on the raised verandah of his van busy lighting the lamps. I also became aware of furtive figures on the lineside close to the stationary train. I saw one reach up to a van door lock which was out of reach, then climb on to his companion's shoulder. Suddenly it dawned on me the train was being tampered with . . .

The signal for the yard remained 'on'; although I could not move towards Niddrie West I still had some latitude in the direction of Niddrie North and the A4 was facing that way. Being braked throughout and tight-coupled, the train moved as a single unit without the buffering-up preliminaries associated with a slack-coupled train. I knew, too, the guard would be prepared for movement – though not the way I planned to go. Drawing my mate's attention to the situation, I quietly 'reversed' the A4 into forward gear, released the brake and gently opened the steam regulator. There was a quiet sustained cough at the chimney accompanied by the desired movement and almost at once the thieves were disturbed and fell to the ground.

After travelling a short distance, I came back to the signal again and, finding it still shut, I continued the to-and-fro movement. The intending robbers were still there, no doubt wondering what was going on but when I came up to the signal for the second time the Niddrie West signalman unknowingly co-operated and pulled it 'off'. As I steamed into the yard the raiders disappeared in the gathering darkness and I duly reported the incident to the railway police. There was no doubt a van had been tampered with and the seal broken but this was renewed and we left Niddrie West on time with the A4 facing miles of open road just as its designer intended. The Niddrie area was notorious for pilfering and it was not uncommon to see urchins clamber aboard moving trains and knock off sizeable lumps of coal which they later gathered and disposed of to their benefit. A Hypermarket has now been built astride the route on which the '5.19' stood waiting and when in this place I smile at the memory of the night I foiled the not-so-great train robbery.

During my early days at St. Margarets I was often involved in coaling engine tenders for through working to Aberdeen where the train crews booked off and rested prior to their return to Edinburgh. The work horse then was the N.B. J37 0–6–0 with a low tender. A wall of coal was built round the tender by the disposal fireman and extra tons of fuel were tipped within and slightly above this wall until the coal was the height of the roof. Latterly, this wall building was dispensed with but it was still necessary for some engines to be well provided for – a three-shift job, for instance, or the double-trip Carlisle.

This latter was one of the hardest jobs at St. Margarets and required a high capacity engine. It was also the most sought-after job and a long night of hard work did not put the men off for the money was enticing. Usually a V2 was allocated to this work and long before the demise of steam these engines and their stable mates were in a sad state of repair, a fact known wherever St. Margarets engines ran. Standing outside the shed, the V2 looked well able to perform but as soon as it started to move a driver's worst fears would be confirmed . . .

Steam erupted from every conceivable point and riding in the cab one got the impression the boiler was positioned over square wheels. On the way up to Waverley Goods, the starting point, worn axle boxes joined in with the 'Gresley Knock' orchestrating a terrific din in the confines of the Calton Tunnel. Emerging into the broad expanse that was Waverley, the locomotive would be more or less obscured by its own steam and smoke and, looking down from the heights near St. Andrews House it seemed as if the twin Calton Tunnels were gun barrels and one had just fired a huge missile, in the form of a V2, with all the ensuing smoke of an explosion. This effect was especially noticeable when the engine emerged from the tunnel at speed.

Drivers of a past era would never have considered leaving the shed with an engine in such a state of disrepair but St. Margarets men had long since learned to live with their inheritance from more efficient depots where better facilities for locomotive maintenance existed. The engines would no doubt be in reasonable shape when transferred to 64A but as common users their condition soon deteriorated and the quick turn round at the depot left little time for repairs. It was not unusual, however, to find that these mobile wrecks were in fact good steamers, which was some compensation for mechanical failing, especially on the demanding Waverley Route.

With their high power and short wheel-base, the V2s were ideally suited to this line through the Border country, which was a gruelling test for engine and men. Long steep inclines to Falahill and Whitrope had to be climbed before a good speed could be reached down Gala Water and through Riccarton Valley. On the return journey there was the long drag through Steele Road to Whitrope Summit and again up Gala Water to Falahill, over 800′ above sea level.

In the darkness of the night, contending with the variations of British weather, enginemen were not inspired as was Sir Walter Scott with the history of Border war and foray or the scenic grandeur of the route. As the V2 blasted its way across the wild terrain, fierce white fireglow flooded the cab and pierced the night sky, occasionally reflecting on the fleece of nearby sheep hurrying away from the frightening sound. In silhouette, the fireman stood firm on the rolling footplate, feeding the hungry flames, while the driver shielded his face from the glare and looked for the signals. Theirs was intensive effort for more than 9 hours, the official diagram being for 9½ hours. They never saw the night shift at St. Margarets, which commenced after their departure and finished before their return. Certainly, no one was more pleased to see Falahill signalbox than the 'double trip' Carlisle men. This marked the end of a night's honest endeavour and from the summit it was more or less 'free wheeling' to the Edinburgh terminus.

Some of the men who drove the 'iron jalopies' that abounded at St. Margarets had style to match the rugged performance of their charges. Others seemed more suited to the refinements associated with Haymarket shed and its 'glamour boy' image. David F. Finaly came into the second category. Davy was of dignified mien, short and portly with a posture not unlike that of the pre-war Aga Khan doing the rounds at Epsom. He was addicted to tobacco and a smouldering cigarette seemed to be a permanent fixture between the nicotine-stained fingers of his left hand which he held against his ample belly. At regular intervals he would brace himself in military fashion and with head held high cast a disdainful look upon his associates, a mannerism that disguised the friendliness he felt towards his fellow men – to whom he was affectionately known as 'Princess Mary'. It seemed Davy was recuperating after being wounded in World War I when King George V's daughter visited the hospital and had the pleasure of meeting Mr. Finaly. Men earned nicknames in St. Margarets for less illustrious tales than the one Davy never tired of telling; little wonder his alias was something special.

He was also unique amongst enginemen, with the letters A.M.I.E.T. after his name and his dialogue on matters technical was far removed from the usual verbal exchanges in the bothy. So many drivers or firemen were just there for the money and in the natural course of events conversation was related to anything but the technicalities of railways.

Jimmy Gibson was another senior driver with a pseudonym aptly suited to his particular manner. In contrast to the feminine gender inherent in Davy's nom de plume, Jim's was pure masculine. Like so many others, it was his utterances that decided his nickname for Jim's pet phrase was "man o' man". While others raved and ranted about a particular unpleasing aspect of the work, Jim would mildly survey the situation and quietly say, "Man o' man, that's terrible." His youthful figure and face belied his age and his rosy cheeks were set in a fixed smile. Only his hat gave a clue to his generation and this he wore square on his head with the top pulled forward over the peak, a style sometimes adopted by younger men who aped their seniors in a friendly jest. "Man o' man" was his own man.

Tommy Glendinning, who in later life was not unlike one of Snowwhite's dwarfs, earned his nickname in a rather amusing way. He and his intended were preparing their wedding feast and Tommy persisted in sampling a dumpling he had a fancy for. Every time he partook of a piece his fiancee scolded him and told him to be patient and wait until the proper time. Long after the festivities were past the loving couple lay in bed, the bride full of passion on this, her 'night of nights'. In the darkness she whispered "Now, Tom, now's your chance." Without hesitation Tom jumped out of bed and grabbed a piece of dumpling. In this way he earned the name Tommy Dumpling and had someone used his proper surname it is doubtful if Tommy could have been identified.

The tradition of nicknames in St. Margarets was as old as the depot itself. There was nothing offensive in this substitution of names; on the contrary, if you had a nickname it meant you were completely accepted, part of the legend.

Most of the workers were family men and Jim Harkins was the daddy of them all. He was father to eleven children and was one of five drivers who came to St. Margarets from Eastfield. Jim was on the coal trains and one fateful day in November 1955 he was driving a J38 0–6–0 on the Glencourse branch. This line is between Millerhill (on the Waverley Route) and Glencorse, situated eight miles away in the Pentland Hills, a place which has for long been the home of the Royal Scots regiment and is now the headquarters of the Lowland Brigade. The passenger train service to the garrison town ended in May 1933 but for many years after goods trains reached this isolated spot over a magnificent viaduct across the Esk valley. In more recent times the railway finished at Bilston Glen where there is a colliery still served by British Rail. Loanhead and Roslin are also on this line.

Depending on requirements, the trip to Loanhead would be by engine and van or with a train of empties. With a good steaming engine the severe gradients were soon overcome, but the descent to Millerhill with a heavy load of coal was a different matter and called for a great deal of skilled driving as well as thorough route knowledge. The guard had to pin down sufficient wagon brakes at the summit near to Straiton Sidings so that the driver could have proper control of the train with the engine and tender brake in reserve plus assistance from the guard's brake as required. More brakes were pinned down at the bridge crossing the Edinburgh to Lasswade road. The difficulty about the Glencorse branch was the levelling out at Gilmerton, half way down, and if the wagon brake power was not overcome by steaming then the whole train came to a stand on this section and brakes had to be lifted and re-applied for the final descent on a 1 in 55 gradient.

It was on this final stretch that Jim Harkins' train ran out of control and, having experienced a 'runaway', I can well imagine his mind's turmoil. With 35 loaded wagons pushing from behind and no means of stopping, a driver can be excused for failing to keep a cool head. His first reaction is to hang on to the whistle, then he is swamped by a feeling of fear and helplessness and his trembling lips could well be murmuring a prayer. More alarming was the real possibility of being diverted into the dead-end dock at Millerhill station, ending up under a heap of smashed wagons and a mountain of coal. There is no way of knowing how the signalman will deal with such a situation; he must protect the main line.

So far as the enginemen were concerned it was now a case of every man for himself. As the J38 rushed on, tender-first, in complete abandon, trailing the bucking coal wagons, Jim Harkins leaped on to a steep embankment and hit the ground with a fierce impact. There was no chance of holding on to the stunted turf and his stunned body slithered downwards on the grassy slope back under the wheels of the raging coal wagons. Death was instantaneous.

The fireman, J. H. Scott, was also injured in his jump a second or two later but was fortunate in sustaining only cuts and severe bruises. He entered hospital some time afterwards, due to an illness in no way connected with the accident and died from natural causes a year later.

The J38 involved in this run-away was equipped with a steam brake, having separate brake cylinders on the engine and tender. The cylinder and the brake hanger beams on the engine were coupled by single pull-rods acting through equalising levers. It was after 1p.m. when Jim Harkins departed from Loanhead and drew slowly towards Straiton Sidings. According to Fireman Scott the train was about to be stopped there to allow the guard to secure a few wagon brakes when a noise from under the engine indicated that some part had broken or given way. On hearing the noise, he climbed from the cab on to the running plate while the engine was still moving, from where he discovered that the brake was no longer effective on the engine, the brake blocks hanging away from the wheels. He returned to the cab immediately and informed Jim Harkins but by the time he had done so the train had begun to gather speed.

The guard was quick to realise that the train was running away: he at once applied his hand brake to the fullest extent but, with no wagon brakes down, he was unable to do more than partially check the train, although Harkins kept the steam brake applied on the tender and opened the regulator after putting the engine in reverse (foregear). The whistle was sounded continuously, which attracted the attention of the porter in charge of Gilmerton station, approximately midway between Loanhead and Millerhill; this man promptly made contact by telephone with Signalman Bell at Millerhill Junction and warned him that the train was out of control.

Bell decided to allow the runaway to pass on to the down main line towards Edinburgh rather than into the dead-ended station dock, where a collision with the buffer stops would certainly have extensively damaged the train, with little hope of the survival of any of the crew who might still be travelling on it, and would have doubtless also damaged the station buildings. An up passenger train was approaching at the time, however, and he very rightly waited for it to clear the junction before setting the points for the down Main. The runaway was within a hundred yards of the points when Bell reversed them to lie for the main line and then lowered the branch line home signal, which he did as promptly as circumstances would allow but by then the enginemen, having seen that their train was apparently about to pass the signal at danger and anticipating a collision with the buffer stops, had already jumped from the footplate. The train passed Millerhill Junction at about 40m.p.h. and eventually came to rest after running a further mile along the down main. The guard remained in his van until the train halted, and it was only then that he became aware that the driver and fireman were no longer on the engine.

It transpired that there had been similar pull-rod fractures on the thirty-five Class J38 engines on previous occasions. They first occurred in 1948 when solid crank shafts were replaced by shafts of the built-up type. There was less clearance under the crank webs of these latter shafts and the brake pull-rods beneath them were offset accordingly but, owing to wear on the axlebox and wheel boss faces, lateral play occurred which allowed the frames to move across the axle, thus bringing the crank web into contact with the brake pull-rod. This ultimately broke owing to repeated blows from the web. To overcome this trouble, the brake gear was re-designed and, commencing in 1953, the necessary alterations were made to these engines as they underwent repairs in the main works. Up to the time of the accident, thirty-one had been dealt with, the engine concerned being one of the four still unaltered. Arrangements were made to fit the modified brake gear to these four engines without further delay.

In the previous year, a no less tragic drama to that which occurred on the Glencorse branch had saddened the railway scene in Scotland. The accident was caused by a defect, but destiny and a measure of indiscipline decreed who the victims were.

An important fitting on the steam locomotive is the baffle plate, or firedoor scoop, as we called it. This was a long shallow scoop designed to be held by the upper lip in the mouth of the firebox, slightly tapered and sloping downwards. Its purpose was to direct air towards the firebed in order to mix it thoroughly with the hot gases and flames. If this plate was not in place, tilted upwards or burnt too short, cold air would pass over the nose of the brick arch to the upper section of the tubeplate, setting up considerable strains in these parts of the firebox, causing leaking tubes, dirty tubeplates and giving poor combustion. To some firemen this was all theoretical nonsense – if they thought about it at all – and if their shovelling was threatened by a long scoop they would lift the plate out and dump it. Some might replace it with a shorter, burnt down version while others made do without. Its sole purpose was as stated and the fitting of a proper baffle plate was part of the self-discipline that management expected of their enginemen. The absence of this fitting seldom caused distress or injury to anyone, but in 1954, a missing scoop indirectly led to the death of two Perth men. This was when Kingmoor engine No.72005 *Clan MacGregor* was hauling the 7.20p.m. Aberdeen to Manchester fish train. It should have been worked forward from Perth by Carstairs men but on seeing it was minus a baffle plate, the Carstairs driver refused to take the engine – and according to regulations right was on his side. Consequently Driver John Lee and Fireman John Lindsay, both of Perth, were detailed to work the train forward while the Carstairs men travelled as passengers. All went well until they passed Auchterarder where a washout plug in the smokebox blew out, resulting in a fierce blow-back into the cab. Both enginemen were very badly burned and the train was brought to a stand at Gleneagles. In sheer agony, the driver carried his mate from the engine and both men were removed to hospital, where the driver died on the 20 February, followed by his mate two days later.

There were ten of these Clans built at Derby in 1952 and more later. Their performance for British Railways was indifferent but generally speaking boilers and washout plugs were never treated with indifference. It was not unusual to have these plugs replaced on the wrong thread after boiler washing but as soon as an engine came into steam this became apparent by a steam blow and the fire was taken out and the engine cooled to allow the plug to be properly fitted. Could it be that in the darkness of the smokebox on *Clan MacGregor* something had gone unseen?

Thankfully, tragic happenings on the railways were, and still are, rare events. Their exceptional nature made them all the more difficult to bear, especially for the railway fraternity. These uncommon occurrences nevertheless served to highlight the importance of teamwork and every man's responsibility to his neighbour. Better design and maintenance could have prevented the untimely death of Jim Harkins, whilst if some boilersmith at Kingmoor had been more attentive the awful accident at Gleneagles would have been avoided. The human element, however, has for long been suspect and on occasions found to be completely wanting. This weakness was in no way strengthened in the years leading up to demise of the steam engine. There was reluctance to spend any money on motive power stock that would become redundant assets in a very short time, so enginemen and maintenance staff had to make-do and mend to a great extent. It says a lot for the powerful ruggedness of the steam locomotive that it was able to perform with reasonable efficiency long after it had been written off. There never has been a nearness between management and staff on the railway and contact and communication is solely through the agency of trade union representatives. In such a big organisation this is understandable to some extent but the remoteness of the two sides encourages apathy and indifference. This situation was aggravated as the condition of the steam engine deteriorated. No one wanted to know about drivers' complaints and a situation developed whereby a discontented engineman was matched with a dilapidated engine, a sure combination for inefficiency.

CHAPTER II

Conditions on shed in steam days – on the brewery branches – night work – temperamental injectors – burned smokeboxes – Portobello shunting yard – a singing guard and his audition – the Corstorphine branch – high speeds at Turnhouse – rules and whistle codes – arguments with signalmen – L.N.E.R. and L.M.S.R. whistles contrasted – diagrams and engines

THOSE WHO cherish the romance of steam must not know of its less pleasing aspects and have never worked in a place like St. Margarets. It was always a dismal environment but on a Sunday night, when engines had just been kindled, the cold boilers and black reek made it even more depressing. The shed was one huge gas chamber and men avoided it until the engines were in steam and the air cleared to some extent. Steam raisers and firemen on kindling duties were prominent as they carried shovels of fire from the sand kiln furnace to the engine being kindled. These shovels had long stout wooden shafts with a metal wall built round the blade in order to form a kind of bucket.

The furnace was too hot to face up to so the kindler turned his back on the fire and pushed the shovel backward into the hot coals. The load was then hoisted on to his shoulder and carried to a particular engine. After placing the shovelful of fire in the cab, the kindler would climb up and deposit the red cinders in the firebox. Usually, the bars were covered with coal and after laying the kindling on this foundation more coal was added. Scores of empty engines were being lit up at the same time, so one can imagine the ensuing smoke.

The air was clearer outside the shed even when the weather was foul. In the crane road and coal road, long lines of Pacifics, K3s and B1s were shrouded in the reek issuing from the fire doors as well as the chimneys. If, for any reason, one had to venture into one of these cabs it was most unpleasant – to say the least. The smoke might suddenly ignite as air from the ashpan and chimney found its way into the fire-box, where it mixed with the smoke and created combustion. A long flame would then leap out into the cab to scorch the unwary.

Looking for kit under these conditions was a distasteful task. Apart from the smoke, tool boxes were in a deplorable state and usually half-filled with slurry (coal dust and water). The tool bucket might be propped up on two firebricks while spanners and detonators lay fast in the mud. Coal hammers and fire irons were often half buried in coal along with firing shovels. All was in darkness, with only the intermittent flames from the firebox to pierce the gloom. One required a flare lamp to see what he was looking for and guard against injury.

As the shed roads cleared, engines outside had to be brought in for preparation. These were coupled together in the darkness but little thought was given to the danger in the work and flare lamps were seldom used. A prudent few provided themselves with battery torches but mostly men worked in the dark guided only by lights on the north side, their glow filtering through the wheels and between engines. There was little chance of seeing any obstruction on the line and it was not until the engines were on the move that a crunch or a lurch would alert the shunters and loud shouting brought the movement to a halt.

While the big shed looked like a disaster area, what remained of the old round shed on the north side of the main line was also a squalid sight. The small shunting engines were stabled there – J83s, J88s and Y9s and these also contributed to the smoke nuisance as their boilers generated steam. It wasn't until about 4a.m. that this place seemed to come to life and aged drivers in various stages of decrepitude could be seen slowly moving about on preparation work. After the wee tankies had been prepared in a lye open to the sky, the turntable was brought round to release these engines from their isolation. On being turned out into the straight it remained only for water to be taken on, then the fireman would cross the main line to the telephone and advise the signalman his engine was ready to leave from the north side. The location was important because the signalman had no way of knowing where the engines were. Shunting engines destined for Leith, Granton, Portobello and Niddrie were usually released via the Bell Lye (so called because of the fire bell position above) and this allowed them to run independently of the main line to Piershill Junction. In this way congestion on the shed was relieved and the Pugs were making headway in the right direction, clear of the main line. At the opportune moment the signalman at Piershill would cross the wee engine to its respective route. Those going in the Portobello and Joppa direction could be run to these points on the 'Slow' road which kept the main line free for more important traffic. Where possible, engines would be coupled together to reduce line occupancy.

Variety is the spice of life and for the spare link man at St. Margarets life had many flavours. In one week he might sample fast freight working, slow passenger trains, coal trains, local trip trains and the menial dock or brewery Pug as well as shunting on N15 0–6–0s in the numerous yards in and around Edinburgh. He soon had a wide knowledge of railway work and came to know a multitude of personnel associated with this work. If one didn't like a particular job there was the consolation of knowing it was just for a limited period. On the other hand, if the work was congenial the spare man could always hope for an extended stay. Apart from the work, there was the change of mates to look forward to or the prospect of earning more money with the travelling time and/or overtime.

Many young firemen were matched with elderly drivers and were generations apart. Add to this the possibility of an ageing driver being in poor health and irritable and you have the mixture for eight hours of misery for a young fireman. Consequently it was all work and no fun in the close confines of the engine cab. It was a welcome change for the fireman when the elderly driver was replaced by a young spare man and life took on a new meaning. The regular driver's strict routine would be varied and everything became more relaxed.

Most of the Pugs at Leith and local breweries were manned by drivers who had been put on them for health reasons. Tommy Hogg was such a driver, being a victim of diabetes. He had to inject himself with insulin at regular intervals and, prior to proceeding to St. Leonards for the second shift of the pilot there, he used to sit in the canteen with all his medical gear on the table dosing himself. At St. Leonards his mate would dose himself with something else – a glass of whisky from the bond and a pint of beer from the brewery.

This was the recognised practice at St. Leonards, which was served by a single line from Duddingston Junction on the Suburban railway. It was originally the Edinburgh terminus of the Edinburgh & Dalkeith Railway, opened in 1831 and closed in 1860. At a particular time each day the driver, fireman and guard would take it in turn to visit the brewery and the bond for their daily ration. I was an innocent abroad when I first learned the ropes at St. Leonards. Sitting on the old J88 one morning my mate said to me, "Are you not going for your pint, Charlie?" Trying to hide my inexperience and at the same time wanting to be 'manly', I feigned indifference and replied "Oh, there's no hurry." Eyeing me somewhat strangely, my mate continued, "If you're not up that ladder at five to nine, you won't get any beer." He obviously knew I was strange to the job and pointed to an iron ladder fixed to the wall of the brewery. "Just climb that ladder," he said, "and up in the loft where the beer is stored there is a barrel tapped and on a trestle. Help yourself with the measure provided."

As I left the engine I thought to myself, "This is some set-up – five to nine – climb a ladder!" a most unusual time and place to have a drink. At the top of this ladder I walked through an opening into a large room with stacks of barrels all over the place. Immediately to my right I saw the barrel on the trestle and a brewery worker helping himself at the tap. I merely followed suit as if I had been drawing and drinking beer all my life and soon I was standing there drinking alongside the brewery man who, by the size of him, had obviously been drawing beer for a very long time. "You just made it," he said, "it's nearly nine o'clock." My facial expression must have been questioning his statement and he went on, "That's the opening hours here – five to nine o'clock." After drinking my quota I descended the ladder feeling somewhat bagged up and decided there and then there would be no more five minute sessions for me.

We carried on shunting in the yard until just after twelve when my mate said, "Are you going for your dram, Charlie?" "Dram!" I exclaimed, "Don't tell me you get whisky here too." Pointing towards the bond he said, "Just go through that door and straight ahead, then slightly to your left there is another door. Tell the man in there you have come for your dram."

Following my mate's instructions, I went through the main door then forward to a 'T' junction where there were other doors facing. I opened one of these and walked in, being surprised to see a naval officer. "What are you looking for, son?" he asked. "I've come for my dram," I replied. "You'll get that next door," he told me after a slight pause. I obviously hadn't veered left enough and after a quick retreat went in next door. In this room there was a man in civilian dress and, seeing my railway clothes he knew without asking what I was after. Taking a large decanter of whisky from a big steel cupboard he poured nearly a half pint into a glass. "Good health," he said as he handed me that generous measure and stood watching. If only I could have poured it into a bottle and taken it home someone would have appreciated it, but there was no escape. I had to drink the stuff there and then. Being the novice I was, it tasted like bad medicine to me and my mouth and throat burned, but bravely I managed to empty the glass. "Thanks," I managed to say, as I left the room. "That was great!" Outside in the yard when the cool air hit me, it looked as if the wagons were shunting themselves. I could feel the whisky tingling the parts other drinks never reach and by the time I got back on the engine I was feeling good. "Did you enjoy that?" asked my mate. "Great!" I replied. "Great!" And I really meant it. "But who is the naval officer?" I asked. "Naval officer!" exclaimed my mate, and suddenly it dawned on him who I was referring to. "That's the Customs & Excise man. Don't tell me you asked him for a dram!" That's exactly what I had done and he had seemed not at all concerned.

The St. Leonards pilot shunted coal and whisky and other merchandise, including beer, of course, but it was the St. Leonards Goods that worked the traffic to and from the yard. Being a light railway set in the Queen's parkland in the shadow of the hill known as Arthur's Seat, only locomotives with a light axle load were suitable for this line. The Class J35, or 'B' as we called it, was the type supplied by St. Margarets.

The single line to St. Leonards was on a rising gradient of 1 in 30 which continued through a tunnel immediately before reaching the yard, where there was a road across the mouth of the tunnel. There was a set of catch points about 100 yards from the top of the incline. This kind of layout called for careful handling of trains and on the first run in the morning when the rails were greasy it was a tricky business.

The authority to occupy this line was No.2 Train Staff (colour white) which had an Annett Key attached for operating the points at each end of Cairntows Loop Siding within the branch. With a good head of steam the driver would start off from Duddingston in the wee valve with the lever back about two notches. As the train speed increased, the lever would be brought farther back and the big valve opened. By this time the exhaust barks were echoing from the hills, smoke rocketed to the sky and the hot fire danced in rhythm with the bouncing engine.

Soon the rollicking train disappeared in the tunnel, its heavy exhaust rebounding from the roof, engulfing train and crew alike. The light at the end of the tunnel was not far distant and here the whole convulsive effort had to be brought under control and smartly stopped clear of the road. Failure to hold the train on the incline meant derailment at the catchpoints and this had to be kept in mind. It's just as well the drink was available at the top of the incline and not at the bottom – although there was plenty there, too, in the numerous breweries at Duddingston.

This brewery settlement on Edinburgh's suburban railway was also the point where assistance was available for heavy trains going north and west. This was necessary to overcome the rising gradient to Morningside Road. The St. Margarets men who manned these assistant engines, usually J35s, were accommodated in an old carriage body, an N.B. inheritance. Such bothies were to be found in a lot of railway yards in Scotland and, although the compartment windows were still in place, the inside seats and partitions had been replaced by long seats against the carriage walls. In the middle of the floor opposite a specially made door marked 'ENGINEMEN' there was a stove and plenty locomotive coal to keep it going. A primitive desk was secured to the wall for the use of drivers writing up their train journals or for signing-on purposes. There was also a notice board giving information about speed restrictions and matters in general affecting railway operations. The 'Water' notice was a very important advice to drivers, this preparatory intimation disclosing where the supply of water had been cut off or restored depending on the maintenance work of engineers. There were two code words used to differentiate and these were 'Boyne' and 'Clyde'. The former meant there was no water and the latter indicated the supply had been restored. It was only necessary to insert a code word along with the date and the location on the ready printed notice.

Because of its compactness and red-hot stove, the ancient bothy soon became overheated but it was a welcome retreat to enginemen who had been exposed to cold weather. After a few runs to Morningside Road on the night shift when traffic was heaviest, it was nice to lie down in the comforting warmth. It was also very easy to fall asleep and lose touch with reality – a telephone alert from the signalman and the vibration felt as a train ground to a halt nearby waiting for assistance. One cold driver at Duddingston, fully aware of his own human feelings and the lost world his young fireman escaped to – put his faith in the bothy cat. He trained this feline creature to lick his face and revive him to wakefulness whenever his services were required.

Working nightshift and attending for duty in the small hours is contrary to nature. Physical power is sapped and drowsiness is a warning that cannot easily be overcome. One might think that driving a steam engine would discourage rather than induce sleep but my experience proved the opposite. Yard shunting is very monotonous work and the perpetual to-and-fro movements plus the heat of the fire had the effect of making me languid. Sometimes it was difficult to respond to the green and red lights displayed by the shunter on the ground and I yearned for the chance to go and lie down – anywhere.

This sleepy feeling could also overtake me on slow banking duties and it could be frightening when the engine was not coupled to the train ahead. The beat of the exhaust and the fire heat acted like a sedative and, leaning on the rocking reversing lever, I often felt my head drooping. Quickly I would shake myself back to life and sometimes find we had lost touch with the train I was supposed to be assisting. A smart 'sprint' would very soon close the gap and the shock was enough to keep me awake after that. Ultimate proof of the danger of man's involuntary surrender to sleep was painfully clear to me one early Sunday morning when I was cycling home from work. It was a five mile journey and the streets were empty. About a mile from home, at a place called Nether Liberton, I actually dozed off in the saddle and was rudely awakened when my bike mounted the pavement and scraped along the side of a wall . . . Enhanced payment for night shift work was well-earned I always thought, and I am now convinced the best place to spend a night is in bed.

Of course, there was not much chance of falling asleep on an engine at the head of a train moving at a reasonable speed. Invariably a driver had to put his head out of the window if only for the purpose of seeing the signals. Even when the front cab windows were clean I preferred signal sighting through open space rather than through glass. At night all kinds of lights were reflected on the cab windows and on some Gresley engines these were angled in an attempt to eliminate 'throw back'. There were eye protector glasses on the side of many cabs but at St. Margarets just as many engines were without such extras. With or without, the driver's head was usually outside the cab except in the most inclement weather. This was the situation when everything was going right but very often everything would go wrong and the image of a driver sitting sedately at the controls was something far removed from realism.

A driver had to be practical when things went amiss and if, for instance, there was a shortage of steam, a reasonable man would not sit with his head out of the window while his mate struggled with the fire.

Very often the fireman sat on the driver's seat out of the way while the driver used his experience for a spell to maintain steam pressure. The struggle for steam could be aggravated by a bad injector. It is just as well there were two of these, although it was not unknown for both to pack up; then it was all fire out – and quick! The larger engines were fitted with an exhaust injector on the fireman's side and a live steam injector on the driver's side. As its name implies, the exhaust injector was worked by steam which might otherwise go up the chimney and was economical in fuel and labour. The smaller 'J' class had two live steam injectors, their design being an inheritance from the N.B.R. These were as good as any others of the same sort but it is their failings that I recall.

The most common one was heating up, which happened when the feed water was too hot or the boiler clack didn't seat properly, allowing steam to blow back. The latter defect could sometimes be remedied by a smart knock in the right place, preferably with a piece of wood – a brake stick, for instance. The whole injector body and the water delivery pipe would be very hot and it was necessary to introduce cold water into the system to cool it down. This required the removal of the water handle which fitted into the injector body and acted as a kind of tap, controlling the flow of water from the tank to the injector. The water handle was held in place by a nut and washer and their removal was a simple matter. This gave access to the overheated delivery pipe and that is when the fun began.

There was seldom a suitable vessel to transfer the water from the tap on the tender to the injector, so the shovel was used. Running under clear signals with the engine working heavy and the apron plate between engine and tender moving in all directions, it was no easy matter to collect a shovelful of water and deliver it to the injector. Once there, what was left in the shovel had to be introduced to the hot pipe from the side and the space between the injector and cab wall was too limited to accommodate the shovel handle. The job called for a lot of patience and some swear words but it was a relief to hear the injector 'singing' again and the all-important water going into the boiler. If overheating persisted, the removal of the water handle and shovelling of water had to be repeated.

On the Carlisle via Hawick road one dark night en route to Lady Victoria Pit with empty coal wagons, my mate and I were struggling to cool down an injector. We were running under clear signals and the engine was driving itself as we shovelled water to the overheated injector. Occasionally I glanced out to see that everything was in order and the business in hand was forgotten when I saw what seemed to be an Unidentified Flying Object floating through the darkness towards us. The glow became more intense as it came nearer and I realised as we were hurrying towards it that it was, in fact, a train descending from Falahill with the engine's smoke-box door white-hot.

This happened when a smoke-box door was not airtight and air, the all-important means to combustion, entered the smoke box through weak jointing. The hot ashes inside would start to burn like a blacksmith's fire and very soon the outside of the smoke box took on the appearance of a fireball – quite an impressive sight on a dark night. It was barely noticeable during the day but the damage to the smoke box was more readily seen. The door would become warped and the baffle plate inside badly burnt, while the sides of the smoke box were weakened in parts by the heat. Sometimes a new door was put on at St. Margarets but more often than not the damaged parts were painted over and so made presentable.

Such damage was detrimental to good steaming and would possibly be caused in the first place by neglect in cleaning the smokebox. I have often stood in the ash lyes at St. Margarets and watched smokebox doors being opened. Once the dart was released from the crossbar it required one mighty effort to free the door, then an avalanche of hot ashes would fall at the cleaner's feet. When the door was swung wide the interior of the box was often an incredible sight. I have seen ashes built up to the chimney petticoat with a centre passage cleared above the blast pipe. Usually the cleaner would start off by banging the baffle plate inside the door with his shovel and ashes would flow freely from the recess. Emptying a smokebox was a long and tiresome task – and very dirty too. Cleaners usually wore goggles, tied sweat rags round their necks and put cycle clips on their trouser bottoms to keep the dust out. There was some deposit left in the smokebox when the door was closed but if the engine was due a boiler inspection or washout the box had to be thoroughly cleaned for this purpose.

The introduction of the self-cleaning smokebox was a boon to the motive power department and the letters SC on a smokebox door were a welcome sight to disposal men. Unfortunately it came too late in the life of the steam locomotive and many were never adapted with the necessary cages. These arrested sparks and prevented costly woodland fires, having made the smokebox ash harmless before it was blasted from the chimney.

On the footplate conditions were considered normal when the driver sat watching signals whilst the fireman fired 'light and often' and kept water in the boiler. There was no anxiety and no demand for great physical effort. Such tranquillity was the exception rather than the rule with St. Margarets engines and everything that could go wrong usually did go wrong.

On one occasion, I was taking a train of empties to Dalkeith Colliery with the usual J37 – my favourite for coal train working. It was one-handed firing with the N.B. ratchet type door and steam was plentiful as my mate thrust each shovelful of coal deliberately into the white-hot furnace. This performance was ideal so long as the coal was available in reasonable sized lumps but the firing rhythm was interrupted when a large piece of coal blocked the supply from the tender. Somewhat annoyed at this cramping of his style, my mate grabbed the coal hammer and fiercely attacked the offending lump. Standing over it on the swaying tender, he first hit the coal from the top, found he was making no impression on the blockage and so next belted it from the front. Unfortunately, he missed the coal and hit the front of the tank, the hammer head disappearing through a hole in the rusting metal. We had filled the tank prior to leaving Leith and all that water was now gushing forth into the cab. I continued to work with that engine on condition I remained reasonably near a water column and when the tank pressure slackened we drove a bung in the hole (a wooden rail key) and in this way carried on until we returned to the depot.

There were quite a few minor defects on an engine that were not readily seen on shed and one of these was a buckled shovel plate. This would be hidden under umpteen tons of coal and only became apparent after much shovelling. Suddenly, the shovel would strike hard against twisted metal, jarring the fireman's arm and causing much distress plus, occasionally, injury. It was sometimes possible to improvise and lay a temporary plate over the defect but the only real cure was to strip the tender of coal to allow the boilersmith to do a proper repair – and this could take a few days.

Just as a car driver acquires road sense over a period of time, experienced enginemen also react automatically. Good eyesight is essential for the proper interpretation of signals and a driver's hearing had to be 'tuned in' to particular noises during the hours of darkness. Familiar sounds echoing through cuttings and over bridges helped him to identify locations and in the absence of speedometers he had to judge his speed by other means. Fire glare could be a hindrance when sighting signals but it also afforded sufficient light on the lineside to enable a driver to get some idea of how fast he was passing telegraph poles and other fixed objects. Although gauges were available for guidance in braking, the experienced man relied more on the feel of the brake. The fireman, too, appeared nonchalant in his approach to the job but the extra tap as he closed the injector steam handle or the water handle was evidence of his thoroughness as he made sure nothing was going to waste. He knew not only when to start firing but exactly how much coal the fire could consume at one time. If he wanted to see the condition of his fire, all he had to do was place his shovel blade at an angle in the fire door and deflected air would clear a passage through the flames.

Curiously enough, apart from seeing and hearing, a sense of smell was also important to enginemen. In this way they were able to detect a hot bearing while running and on the Gresley three-cylinder engines a fused 'bomb' in the centre big end could cause a real stink. Being remote, this part of the motion was out of reach – hence the warning device to alert the driver to overheating. The released fluid smelt like garlic and this unpleasant odour would remain long after the defect had been put right. For one reason or another a hot bearing could be overlooked and would lose its heat after the engine had been on shed for awhile. More than once I have gone under a three-cylinder engine to oil the centre motions and discovered the boiler bottom and inside framing splattered with white metal. This was an indication that something had fused; a closer examination of the big and small ends would determine where the damage lay. Of course, the finding had to be reported to the running foreman who would curse somewhat before arranging to have the engine shunted out and the fire drawn. Then the problem was to find a replacement and have it prepared in time to take up its diagram working.

The most common cause for late departure from St. Margarets shed was missing kit, any item of which could cause delay – shovel, lamps, fire irons, detonators, red flags, spray pipe, footplate brush, coal hammer, etc. All were portable and easily removed but the time came when even the engine itself was cannibalised and fittings disappeared – injector handles, brake handles, gauge column protectors and footstools. In the beginning the stools were joiner-made and shaped to fit round the faceplate fittings on particular engines. Latterly one could expect an engine to be minus a footstool, consequently an engine of a similar class was robbed to make up the deficiency. When the proper stool was unavailable a length of sleeper or other timber was introduced. Sometimes this wood lay on the cab floor or it could be raised on two bricks depending on the design of the cab. This type of elevated platform caused me to come a cropper one day.

I had just relieved a driver at Portobello and before I had time to take my jacket off the guard waved me back onto the train. The engine reversing lever was fully forward and with one mighty heave I pulled it back for the required direction of travel. Unfortunately, I stood on the outer edge of the elevated platform and as it up-ended under me I fell full length against the tender and slithered on to the apron plate where I sat dazed and amazed, looking rather foolish. My mate roared with laughter and I remained in my undignified position to keep him happy. Meanwhile, the impatient guard came up to the engine to investigate the delay and when he saw me on the floor he said, "Oh! sitting down on the job, eh?" He helped me to my feet and as we moved back on to the train I threw the footstool and supporting bricks overboard, then went in search of a solid piece of wood.

In the hey-day of steam, Portobello and Niddrie West were the two busiest goods yards in the Edinburgh area, with South Leith and Meadows Yard not far behind. I have known these yards at all times of the night and day and in all seasons. During the warm summer weather it was short sleeve order for enginemen and shunters alike whilst meal breaks were out in the open. It was all very different in the depths of winter and especially at night. In my mind's eye I can see again the vast sidings with engine smoke drifting low over hundreds of wagons. There was always intense shunting activity and I remember the rain and snow blowing relentlessly into the shunters' faces. They wore black rubber coats and leggings and sou'westers, each being armed with a hand lamp and shunting pole. Working in pairs, the No. 1 man controlled the points to the various lyes while his assistant uncoupled the wagons being shunted. This was done when the engine buffered up and as the movement quickly accelerated to the urgent waving of the shunter's lamp the uncoupled wagons gained sufficient momentum to take them loosely into the sidings. Should they be moving too fast the man at the points would drop brakes as they sped on their way and his expertise determined a suitable speed on entering the lye.

After disposing of a train at Portobello there was always another one waiting to be shunted. As heavy rain washed over them, the two shunters would climb on to the engine footstep and from my high perch in the cab I used to look down with pity on these wet wretches. The feeble yard lighting only served to emphasise the misery of working under such conditions and the dull glow made visible the downpour which could be felt in the dark lanes between endless rows of wagons.

"Right, Charlie, over to the Centre Road," this from the leading shunter on the footstep. I knew from his instruction what was expected of me and smartly opened wide the regulator and hurried in the direction of the elevated signalbox that was Portobello East Junction. This long signalbox spanned yard sidings and a double main line where the Waverley Route diverged from the East Coast road. In the absence of telephone communication there was a whistle code to alert the signalman and the 'open sesame' for the Centre Road was two long and three short. The noise seemed outrageous in the middle of the night in that densely populated area but this whistling went on for umpteen years with the blessing of railway management.

Once on top of the train we were preparing to deal with the shunters would disappear into the darkness with only their oil handlamps to guide them. In the engine cab we were conspicuous in the firelight and as we waited for the shunters to check the train only a gentle hiss disturbed the stillness of the night. Sometimes when cattle were in transit we could hear their mournful mooing and the sound of agitated hoofs kicking against the wagon sides. One had to be wary when walking near these cattle vans. They oozed muck and this filth, at head level, was constantly being ejected by the restless beasts.

One dark night as I stood with my engine in the Centre Road, I became aware of a strong smell of whisky. I decided to investigate and climbed down into the darkness. Below the engine there was the red glow from the ashpan and beyond the vehicles in the adjacent roads were the yard lights shining through the wheels and between the wagons. On the ground my eyes became accustomed to the shadows and from my position the space below the wagons was clearly seen against the yard lighting, so clear, in fact, that I immediately spotted the source of that intoxicating odour – whisky was leaking from a van. I was sorely tempted to empty my tea bottle and fill it with the precious drink soaking into the ground but I advised the Inspector instead. This worthy immediately alerted the Customs & Excise people who came and dealt with the 'disaster' in their usual efficient manner. After breaking the seal, the van door was opened and torch beams spotlighted a hogshead of whisky lying on its side leaking, the result of bad loading and/or a rough shunt. The Customs men managed to stop the flow and took details of the load before re-sealing the van door.

Just as there were amusing characters in the locomotive grades, the traffic grades also had some comedians in the ranks. One such comic was a guard called Albert Cooper and his party piece was Al Jolson songs. Albert's 'dead-pan' look matched his serious attitude to singing but an observer would liken his unsmiling face to Buster Keaton-style comedy. My first encounter with this popular guard was at St. Margarets when an N15 tank engine came in for coal, hauling a brake van with Albert leaning over the verandah. His mobile stage stopped beside a group of engine disposal men, a captive audience, and they immediately called out for a performance. The entertainer always went for realism and he proceeded to blacken his face with coal dust. As enginemen and fitters gathered round laughing Albert pulled on a pair of new industrial gloves, the best substitute he had for the White gloves that were Jolson's hallmark. In the restricted space on the verandah he could not throw his arms out as wide as he would have liked, so he became a bit lop-sided and took advantage of the space between engine and van. Soon he was putting his whole heart into "Mammy" and, like Jolson was down on his knees with arms outstretched. At this point the coal tipper who had been watching from above decided to lower the tip ready for coaling and in doing so he called out, "If you don't get out of the road, you'll be seeing your mammy in hospital!" Albert was just walking "a million miles for one of your smiles" when the interruption came and without further ado he disappeared into his van. Instead of thunderous applause from his audience he heard the thunder of coal dropping into an empty bunker . . .

Some time later Albert was my guard on the coal trains and at Granton enginemen and shunters planned a surprise for him. Alex Bennet, a St. Margarets driver, who in 1935 I had succeeded as toolstore boy at Haymarket, was the spokesman for this group of pranksters and in serious mood he confronted Albert. "There was a man here tonight from the B.B.C. inquiring about you, Albert. He wants you to make a recording of your act." The guard's mouth opened in disbelief. "He'll be here tomorrow night at 10 o'clock with his recording equipment, so I hope your voice is in good fettle." From then on Albert was up on the engine talking to my mate and me, asking our advice about what numbers to sing for the B.B.C. as well as various other problems that had suddenly arisen in connection with his repertoire. I could not keep my face straight and left it to my mate to help prepare Albert for his big 'audition'.

Next night I was still braking the heavy coal train on the approach to Granton when Albert passed the engine hurrying in the direction of the enginemen's bothy. It was some minutes later when my mate and I followed and, on seeing the crowd in the bothy plus the lavish equipment installed, I began to think A.B. had been serious about the B.B.C. There was, in fact, a well-dressed gent present who would not have looked out of place in a recording studio. I recognised some others as stevedores and fishermen. But where had all the wires and boxes come from; with those flashing lights and microphone, it looked realistic and impressive.

After being formally introduced to the 'B.B.C.' man, Albert listened intently to instructions regarding the recording. This briefing was concluded with some professional advice about relaxing. "Forget about the microphone and concentrate on the audience," said the man wearing the good clothes and looking so refined. "Once I get your voice on tape the background music will be added in the studio – now, are you ready!?" All was still as Albert's shifting eyes ranged over the expectancy in the faces of the audience, whose encouragement became quite unrestrained. His eyes finally focused on the 'B.B.C.' man who appeared to make some adjustment in the equipment and simultaneously signalled by hand for the singing to start. The opening words of "Sonny Boy" reverberated in the confines of that small bothy and, as Albert went on about "not minding the grey skies", heads were bowed and shoulders shook as the audience muffled their giggles. Only the 'B.B.C.' man kept a straight face and at the opportune moment sliced the air with outstretched arms indicating 'finish'. "Right, Albert," he said, "that was great, I'll let you know how the final recording turns out." Just then the bothy door opened and the yard foreman picked out Albert's face. "Are you in charge of that train outside?" he yelled, ignoring all that was going on, and without waiting for an answer continued, "Catch that bloody van and get away back to Lady Victoria." With that one bald statement, Albert's dream world tumbled like coal from a hopper and soon our train was on the climb from sea level towards the pit with the majestic name in the Moorfoot Hills. Looking back from our J37 I could see Albert in the van behind silhouetted against the receding city lights and his gesticulations indicated he was busy at rehearsal for the next show.

I learned later that the elaborate prank at Granton was a result of the combined efforts of railwaymen and trawlermen, the 'B.B.C.' man being, in fact, a trawler skipper. The sophisticated equipment was made up of discarded wireless material and spent batteries from railway telephones.

Some passenger guards were fun to work with and far removed from the serious image of the élite East Coast guards who earned good status by their self-disciplined behaviour and smart appearance. The men in charge of the local passenger trains were less inclined to promote order, regularity or offical obedience. They took the line of least resistance, merely looking for a quiet life. In this respect nothing could be less hectic than the 5.18p.m. Edinburgh to Corstorphine, a very busy local which travelled a distance of about three miles.

Unlike the other suburban trains diagrammed to be worked by St. Margarets engines and men, the '5.18' was the sole job in the diagram. But it was an important one, if only because a great many railway headquarters staff travelled home by this service. The enginemen rostered for this work usually took the first available passenger engine, which could be anything between a J37 and a A4, or occasionally a tank engine. It mattered not what way the engine was turned over such a short distance with three intermediate stops. After the passenger alighted at Corstorphine, the engine rounded the train, which returned to Waverley Station with one headlamp below the chimney (or atop the tender), indicating a stopping passenger train.

More often than not the train was empty and one week when I was on the job the guard spoke to me on the Monday regarding the return working. "As you can see," he said, "this train is empty but I'll be looking out approaching Pinkhill and Balgreen Halt. If there are no passengers on the platform I'll give you a wave so don't bother stopping." Then, apparently as an afterthought, he continued, "You'd better stop at Haymarket, though in case somebody's watching." All this made sense to me, a seemingly pre-arranged 'failure to make a booked stop'. Such a misdemeanour however was, and still is, frowned on by management and the Corstorphine episode was recalled some years later when a driver colleague was asked to explain his failure to make a booked stop. "It's like this," he told the shedmaster, "I knew there was nobody on the train wishing to alight at that station and I could see there was nobody on the platform, so what's the use of stopping?" The boss did not appreciate the logic in this explanation and my driver friend was quietly reprimanded and told to be more careful in future.

Corstorphine was the end of a branch line diverging from the main line at Haymarket West. There was an arrival and a departure platform served by independent lines with a crossover about two engine lengths from the arrival buffer stop. Trains were expected to go as near as possible to the buffer then, after the passengers had alighted, the carriages would be pushed back clear of the cross-over, where the engine was uncoupled for rounding purposes. After recoupling to the other end, the train was moved into the departure platform.

Some of the big engines were less than convenient to shunt with and, in order to minimise the number of movements, it was not unusual for the '5.18' to be stopped short of the crossover. This mean that passengers had a few more yards to walk to the station exit. Being people with some influence on the railway it was not long before a notice went up at St. Margarets instructing all drivers on the '5.18' to stop near to the buffer instead of short of the crossover. Those clerks hurrying home for tea had no consideration for the driver who had to operate a stiff reverser seven times before leaving Corstorphine . . .

Not far from the now defunct Corstorphine branch there is the main line to Fife and the North and I knew this stretch at an early age when, in 1928, I walked with other boys to Turnhouse Aerodrome (now Edinburgh Airport) on a very special occasion. This was to see the plane which had raced from London with The Flying Scotsman.

Apart from childhood sentiments, this stretch of line was always a favourite with me. Turnhouse lies in a hollow and a high speed can be reached in each direction. After the restriction on the Forth Bridge or the slow running out of Edinburgh, a driver was faced with an open stretch of line the gradient and signalling of which allowed for minimum use of the brake. It was a delight to give the engine its head and go blasting into the dip and up the other side. Passenger vehicles would follow steadily behind but wagons with a short wheelbase would roll and lurch as if convulsed. As the speech increased, the crew would rock with the oscillating engine which appeared demented as it stampeded through the open country. This rare sensation could be achieved in many places and it was the building up of momentum rather than the ultimate high speed that imparted vigorous life to the steam engine. As high pressurised superheated steam smacked the piston faces in the cylinders, resistance against the wheels and linked motions was lost on the slight falling gradient and the train's fierce impetus reached a peak as it thundered through Turnhouse.

This lively performance was readily seen in the daytime but at night it was felt even more and only the steam and smoke reflecting in the firelight beam were visual evidence of the engine breathing fire as it rushed through the darkness. I never contemplated sudden misfortune or anything approaching disaster at speed but the possibility was brought home to me when I made an examination of my V2 in the lights at Waverley station one night after working a train from Perth. The right outside motions on the coupled wheels were at platform level and the cotter which secured the eccentric crank, big end and side rod, was missing. Only minutes before, this heavy mechanism had been whirling at tremendous speed with nothing to prevent it from falling apart except the tight fit of the eccentric crank! Being so near to St.

Margarets it was no problem to call a fitter – but had the works come adrift as we raced through Turnhouse we would have required more than that!

Part of a driver's training involved making an engine fit to travel and clearing the main line in the event of the gearing breaking up. How would you deal with a broken piston rod? What would you do if the combination lever broke? All these and many more were questions a man had to answer before he became a driver and in theory it all seemed useful knowledge. But, thankfully, I never had to practise any of it. Can you imagine attempting to disconnect valve gearing or other parts of the motion with only a gauge column key and a coal hammer – which is about all St. Margarets engines ever carried in the way of tools. If an engine broke down in traffic the crew was more concerned about protecting the train than effecting repairs; it was easier to call out the tool van.

Rules were also an important part of an engineman's training and instructions in the use of Wrong Line Orders had to be learned. As the name implies these authorised wrong line movements and could be issued by driver, guard or signalman depending on the circumstances. The four forms were identified by colour and a letter A, B, C or D. The drivers had Form B which was green and this was usually kept in the rule book in the breast pocket, seldom seeing the light of day. Its purpose was to allow an assisting engine to occupy the same line as the defective engine it was going to assist. In the event of failure the driver would complete Form B, then this was taken to the nearest signalbox in advance by the fireman. This form authorised the signalman to allow an assisting engine into the section on the wrong line. The responsibility for being in possession of Form B was that of the driver but only the more conscientious men bothered about such details. Like the steam engine on British Railways, these forms are now part of railway history.

Just as wrong line order forms belong to the past, so the whistle code is a bygone contemporary of the steam engine. This means of communication between drivers and signalmen covered a wide range of matters. The primary use of the code was for routeing trains but there were whistles for water, banking assistance, lineside fires, brake assistance from the guard, train out of control plus warning signals for men on the line, level crossings or tunnels. There is still a need for warning signals with modern traction but today's driver is less concerned with routeing and water. The code came easily to drivers working on the same line over long periods but to the uninitiated it had to be learned, along with many other things. Sometimes the regular driver or conductor was not conversant with a particular whistle and more than once when I have asked for guidance the conductor in his ignorance would say, "Oh, give him a handful – he'll sort them out." This meant that the signalman would hear a jumble of sound instead of distinct notes and only his experience would tell him what was required. It was important to use the whistle code at the proper locations so that the signalman ahead could be advised of the requirement. For instance, a driver was not expected to wait until he was at a junction before he routed himself. When given prior warning from the box in the rear the junction signalman could possibly have the route set for the approach of the train, thus avoiding delay.

Sometimes a driver would become dependent on the signalman's alertness and experience and neglect to sound the whistle. More often than not no harm was done but occasionally a signalman would stick to the regulations and make an issue of the whistle code. This would result in the signal being against the driver on the train's approach and after braking to a stop, or near stop, the signal would be pulled off slowly. This allowed the train to move forward to the box where the signalman was leaning from his window. The driver would stop and look up at the man and the following conversation might ensue. "Where are you going?" says the signalman. "I'm not a mind reader, you know." "Fine you bloody ken where I'm going!" replies the driver as the safety valves erupt into the signalman's face. "Keep that bloody engine quiet," retorts the irate leverpuller as he belatedly withdraws into the box, emerging again when the steam pressure subsides. "In future," he yells to the driver, "route yourself and you'll maybe get somewhere," turning away to pull the necessary levers. Turning to his fireman, the driver says, "If I go up there I'll route him, and he'll get somewhere – to the damned cemetery!"

This was the kind of attitude that created enmity and contributed nothing to railway business. Sometimes the ill will between driver and signalman would persist and they would 'have it in' for each other. The signalman had it in his power to delay a driver at a time when the latter was looking forward to an early finish or a clear run. The driver on the other hand could wait his chance and report the signalman for any irregularity, no matter how slight. It was a situation to be avoided but, human nature being what it is, this clash of personalities was not unusual. The possibility of such incidents occurring today is less likely although telephone wires sometimes become overheated with verbal abuse as a driver on the lineside phone lets fly at his unseen tormentor in some remote signalling centre or Control room.

L.N.E.R. steam engines in general had a feeble whistle – and none at all if the boiler water level was high. The L.M.S. Black Fives and 8Fs, W.D. Austerities, B.R. Standards and Gresley A4 were the engines I preferred for whistling. Their deep-throated bass sound carried far, was clear, and commanded attention. The two cock crows exchanged by a train engine and its banker could be quite a contrast in sound if there was a shrill whistle answering the deep fog-horn, or vice versa. At places like Craigentinny Carriage Sidings there were regular 'musical' interludes as locomotives prepared to take a heavy lift of carriages up the 1 in 78 to Waverley station. The 'banker' would be attached to the rear of the train by coupling only (no brake or heater pipes) with the steam regulator off the face and the buffers compressed. When the signal came off, the train driver would sound two cock crows simultaneously to opening the throttle. As the train moved forward the banking engine would automatically move gently with it because of the steam applied, while the driver answered with two cock crows on the whistle, an assurance to the man up front that he was being assisted. If there was a clear road to the Waverley, the train would have built up some speed by the time it raced through St. Margarets before steadying up on the incline beyond the tunnel. Most drivers gave a long warning whistle on the approach to 64A and this is where the fog-horn type could be heard to advantage.

The Class V1 tank engine was the most popular type for empty coach working and the fire made up at Craigentinny was sufficient for the trip to Waverley. This left the driver and fireman free to wave to colleagues at St. Margarets or people in the houses in that area. Sometimes a high capacity engine en route to Haymarket Shed was utilised to work empty coaches and this could be seen, usually tender-first, making an effortless run up the hill to Waverley. After uncoupling, it was suitably placed for a quick release to Haymarket.

There were diagrams for passenger and freight trains, these being posted in their respective cases at the depot. Drivers who were on regular link work usually copied these diagrams in a notebook which was convenient for their progress through the link from week to week. Of course, one had to check for alterations in the booked working and it was not unusual for a driver to be caught out in this respect. For instance, an inspector at Craigentinny might become concerned regarding the non-appearance of a particular locomotive and advise Control to this effect. On checking with signalboxes and other sources the errant driver would be found at Waverley working to the sequence of events detailed in the diagram before it was altered. Sometimes it was too late to rush the 'lost' engine to Craigentinny and alternative arrangements had to be made. Because of personal needs and the limits thus imposed, enginemen could not match the availability of their engines so there had to be separate diagrams for the men and their machines.

When a particular class of engine was not available for diagrammed work another type would be utilised. So far as the running foreman was concerned it was an engine and the job was covered. Little thought was given to the men who had to work with the engine. It might be quite unsuitable for manoeuvring in limited spaces or signal sighting could be affected. Shunters, too, would complain about not having a suitable footstep to ride on and difficulties in coupling. Then there were steam blows to contend with, a common hindrance to visibility, whilst if an engine fitted with a snowplough appeared on the scene the shunters could not be blamed for refusing to work with such a hazard. It was, therefore, an advantage for a practical man to be doing running foreman's work. A man who had seen it all outside knew at once what was required when allocating power. He knew the demands of a particular job as well as the capabilities of certain engines; this all added up to experience, a priceless asset.

I had won this valuable commodity by hard work in the motive power department over many years. I had experienced most of the work associated with the steam engine and had known that temperamental machine in all stages of dress and undress, from the gleaming elegance of the Haymarket stud to the drab workhorses that abounded at St. Margarets.

CHAPTER III

Running foreman – development of Thornton – Thornton shed – the staff and the locos, steam and diesel – a damaged Class 37 diesel-electric – shed personalities – railcars – an attempted suicide – a derailed Austerity – the log book – 'keep the wheels rolling'

MY PREVIOUS VOLUME, *L.N.E.R. Footplate Memories*, covered only part of the memorable years I spent as a locomotiveman. Worthwhile as it was, driving trains was not the ultimate in job satisfaction so far as I was concerned. More challenging to me was the Running Foreman's job at St. Margarets or Locomotive Inspector at Waverley Station. In these positions I took on a far wider responsibility and became more involved with railway work and personnel. The never-ending demands of such work kept me occupied and that's the way I liked it.

I was on supervisory work for long periods before I was permanently appointed running foreman at Thornton, Fife. Instead of the latter, it might have been Corkerhill, Glasgow, Dundee or Aberdeen or my home depot, St. Margarets. Over the years I applied for supervisory work at many places, but it was George Luttrell, the superintendent located at Thornton, who opened the door for me.

There are always interviews preceding appointments and in my experience some of them were a waste of time. Sometimes an interview was worthwhile and the superintendents and their assistants probed deeply. This was the case at Edinburgh when I went after a supervisors' job at St. Margarets. Ex-Royal Engineer Colonel R. Thomson was the District Motive Power Superintendent and he covered a lot of ground during the interview.

Apart from rules and regulations and railway matters in general he dealt thoroughly with running foreman's work. At one stage he asked me how long it would take me to have an engine in steam after boiler washing. I was not trying to impress him when I said, "Possibly two hours". This was a fact of life in St. Margarets when a medium-sized engine off washing out was filled with hot water and kindled. "What!" said the Colonel, "do you realise the damage that can ensue by forcing steam in such a short time?" Before I could say anything about the strain on the boiler and firebox caused by rapid expansion, the Colonel leaned across his desk and quietly said, "Two hours, eh? If you can do it as quickly as that, then carry on!" However, I was destined to perform my amazing steam-raising act at St. Margarets solely in my capacity as Acting Running Foreman. It was not until July 1963 that the interview leading to my appointment as Running Foreman took place at Thornton.

The District Motive Power Superintendent there was responsible for motive power activities between Forth Bridge North and Dundee, being located in offices at Dormitory House near Thornton shed. This 'sleeping chamber' was so called because the building had once been used for trainmen on book-off jobs.

The interviewing panel confronting me included the superintendent George Luttrell, who was flanked by his assistant George Cherry and Thomas F. Mackay, the shedmaster.

This was my first meeting with Mr. Luttrell and Mr. Mackay but I knew Mr. Cherry who had previously been shedmaster at St. Margarets.

All three men were mechanically trained. Mr. Luttrell had served his apprenticeship at St. Rollox and had a wide experience of steam locomotive and railways before coming to Thornton. Mr. Cherry had been a fitter at Carlisle about the time I was on cleaning there, whilst Mr. Mackay hailed from the North Eastern Region and at that time was to me an unknown quantity.

The interview lasted more than an hour, although the discourse that I was involved in made me oblivious to time. Mr. Luttrell just about covered the lot, including the maximum line speed between Edinburgh and Dundee. When he stopped for breath, his colleagues quickly took over and in the end I felt my journey from Edinburgh had really been worth while. Somehow, I had the feeling that something would come of this interview but I was, nevertheless, surprised and delighted when a letter to my home advised me that I had been appointed Running Foreman at Thornton with effect from 12 August 1963.

As in many other instances, the village of Thornton is far removed from the railway station, which in 1963 was known as Thornton Junction. This was situated on the main Edinburgh to Aberdeen line. I was no stranger to this part of Fife having often worked into Thornton from Edinburgh. It was near enough the half-way mark between Edinburgh-Dundee and was handy for engine replacements en route. If, for instance, something went wrong with an engine after leaving Edinburgh, the driver would advise the signalman at Forth Bridge North, say, and word would be passed to the Control who would arrange for a change of engine at Thornton.

The Thornton I came to for promotion was formed around the village of the same name in 1877, which originally owed much of its growth to a number of small coal-pits worked at the south end – Ore Bridge as it was then called. With the steady development of the railway system, Thornton's position at a cross-roads of natural communications took on a new importance.

By the end of the nineteenth century four separate lines converged on Thornton station, so that the comparatively small village quickly found itself on the map as an important railway junction. It became, and remained, largely a railway town. Before long a shed with four roads to hold 30 locomotives had been built, while extra platform space had to be provided, the station enlarged and waiting rooms built. Over the years it has been a never-ending battle to keep these buildings above ground owing to mine workings in the area. These same excavations made it necessary for a permanent speed restriction to be enforced. The N.B.R. used to have a small gas plant here for the use of station and shunting yards and a loading bank plus a goods shed were also in use.

In 1923 a wagon repair works was erected near the old engine shed for repair of the railway's own rolling stock. Two private firms had built wagon repair shops in 1898 and these were still in operation just prior to my arrival at Thornton.

In 1933, a new shed was built at the west end of Thornton to hold 100 modern steam locomotives of all kinds. It was opened by Miss Whitelaw, daughter of the L.N.E.R. chairman at that time, and there was a plaque outside the general office to indicate this.

The new Rothes Pit opened by the Queen in 1956 was across the main line from Thornton shed, its winding towers standing up like two fingers. This ultra-modern pit held much promise for work in the area and Glenrothes new town was built on the strength of that promise. It was estimated that there would be an output of one million tons of coal a year, giving employment to two thousand men. But this was not to be and all that remains of Rothes Pit is two massive concrete skeletons and a large heap of waste close to where Thornton shed used to be. Deep in the bowels of the earth, the rich coal seams lie waterlogged.

The approach to Thornton Shed was by a flight of steps leading from the Thornton/Kirkcaldy A92 road. These steps were adjacent to the bridge carrying the road over the branch line to Cowdenbeath and Dunfermline. At the foot of the steps, to the left, there was Dormitory House and close to the District Headquarters there was a wooden army hut used for ambulance meetings and, at one time, social activities. Beyond this hut, rails which once served a wagon repair shop were embedded in the road which ran parallel to the main line.

Half-way along the road to the shed the Weighs signalbox stood on the other side of the shed outlet lines on the right. Ahead was the turntable which could be reached with the signalman's permission through the facing road or in the proper direction from the south side of the shed.

Beyond the turntable, on the left, were the general offices and lecture rooms. The shedmaster also had his office in this block. Stepping over the rails leading from the south side of the shed to the turntable one came to another ex-army hut used as a canteen. Directly in line with this was the running office which shared a porch with the enginemen's bothy. The cleaners' bothy was adjacent to the latter.

Outside the doors to these premises a single line served the material store, the rails being flush with the ground. This area was flanked by the bothy wall and the shed wall while the store access doors made a third wall, so that there was a kind of alcove with the engine board and notice boards fixed to the walls under bright lights. This was the running foreman's territory. If drivers and firemen were not given instructions elsewhere they very often got to know what was expected of them beside the engine board.

The single line to the store passed by the front of the running office and canteen and this line was used to stable standby engines, usually a couple of B1s.

Emerging from the running office, the front of the shed lay straight ahead and, after crossing six shed roads, one came to the engine disposal area where stood the coaling plant and ash lyes. Engines would come in past the Weighs signal box then, after being coaled, they moved on to the wet ash pit for fire, ashpan and smokebox cleaning. Half way along this inlet road there were holding points which allowed engines to bypass disposal and proceed into the road between the shed and disposal lye, where there was also a loop line.

This road was known as the 'Fat Wife', a most unusual name even for railway colloquialism. The story goes that in far-off days an engine named after some obese female once stood in this road and when the time came to position another engine the supervisor told the driver to "Pit it on top o' the fat wife". Ever since then this particular road was known as the 'Fat Wife'.

When diesel rail cars were stabled at Thornton shed a fireman stood waiting at the holding points to let them run direct into the 'Fat Wife', thus bypassing the coaling plant and disposal lyes. His was a cold job in

Thornton D49 No.62729 *Rutlandshire* at home in the ash-lye. Access to the pit is by steps immediately below cab and protected by a low wall. Grab crane in the background worked during the day to load ashes into adjacent wagons which went to the Kelty Coup. [Brian Morrison]

the winter and there was always a glowing brazier to comfort him.

From disposal, engines went to the west end of the shed where they were admitted to a particular shed road. If one had to be turned it was necessary to go to the western extremity of the yard where there was a shunt spur and from there down past the south side of the shed to the turntable. After turning, the engine would return by the same route and enter the west end of the shed. In all, the distance covered would be about half a mile.

Entry to the fitting shop and drop pit was also at the west end and, adjacent to a running loop line, on a large expanse of ground, there was a short loop where diesel locomotives and rail cars were fuelled. This loop held nine rail cars. Also in this grassy area there was storage space for oil barrels. Close to the shed there was a single line and here stood the steam locomotive that acted as stationary boiler for washing out purposes. Holmes J36 65345, the last steam engine to serve B.R. in Scotland was often a stationary boiler at Thornton.

A wartime innovation at Thornton was unique in Scotland. This was the 'light tunnel' introduced by the L.N.E.R. – a floodlit artificial tunnel which enabled engines to be examined quickly and without difficulty during the blackout. It was 80′ long and had whitened walls on which were fitted fluorescent lighting tubes. Between the track there was a white glazed brick inspection pit embodying alcoves in which there were further lighting units. There were larger doors at each end of the tunnel and a master switch cut off the main lighting as soon as these were opened. This tunnel was adjacent to the inlet road and ash lyes; appropriately, Thornton men called it the 'snake pit'.

Last, but not least, there was the steam breakdown crane which was stored near coal sidings between the coaling plant and the Weighs signalbox, adjacent to the main line. The location of the crane at Thornton gave the depot status, also the number 62A while the important Dundee depot had to be content with 62B.

The topography of Thornton motive power depot had long been known to me but what about the biography of its personnel? Every man was an unknown quantity to me, and me to them. Many years before my appointment at Thornton, supervisors from St. Margarets used the Fife depot as a step to promotion at their home depot. Jimmy Brown, Jimmy Graham and Andrew Black had all served at Thornton before reaching senior posts at St. Margarets.

I was quite looking forward to a change of abode and went with my family to live at Glenrothes. While crossing the Forth Bridge we looked down on the ferry boat at Hawes Pier and there was Pickfords removal van taking all our worldly goods to the New Town. I, of course, had been working at Thornton before my family moved north. My first week there was on the day shift and my tutors were George Shand and his assistant Willie Young, alias 'Darky'.

Willie was about ages with me and our seniority was similar. He told me he acquired his nickname when, as a young cleaner, he was under an engine and his face became black with oil. Ever since then he was affectionately known as Darky. Truth to tell, the fact that his skin pigment could be likened to an Arab might also account for the nickname.

It was Willie's job I had to learn before taking up my own position on another shift. Just as he was assistant to George Shand, I was eventually to go on with Dave Leitch. The running foremen on the third shift were Dave Thomson and Charlie Beattie, while Harry K. Brown was the relief running foreman.

Compared with St. Margarets, Thornton was a rest home. There was more room to manoeuvre and a through shed to work with. The coaling plant and wet ash pits were a real advantage, also one could foresee busy spells and slack periods. St. Margarets, on the other hand, had always been hustle and bustle, muddle and confusion, 24 hours a day.

Although there were less of them, the types of locomotives at Thornton were the same as St. Margarets, without the high capacity engines. There were W.D. Austerities working trains to Aberdeen via Coupar Angus, as well as by way of Dundee. The J37s and Fife's own J38s dealt with local traffic while B1s were ready for almost anything. Just as St. Margarets men felt affection for the Y9 68119, Thornton men had a regard for the veteran J36 65345, which for a long time assisted trains on the Cowdenbeath branch and was known as the 'hill pilot'.

There were also sufficient diesel units to justify construction of fuel sidings, along with two large storage tanks and pump house. During the night Nos. 1 and 2 roads were filled to capacity with rail cars. These were fuelled prior to stabling, then marshalled and prepared for their next workings. There were also 350hp E.E. shunters and four-coupled Hunslets to serve sub-depots at Thornton New Yard, Ladybank, Markinch, Methil, Kirkcaldy and Burntisland. This mixture of steam and diesel was far from ideal but such was the situation pending improved arrangements. The first allocation of main line diesel locomotives came to Thornton in 1966 in the form of English Electric Type 3 No.6859.

Some Thornton men had already been trained to drive main line diesel locomotives as well as the shunters and rail cars. A driver's qualifications to drive a particular type of diesel traction were entered on his route card, the card he signed twice a year, in March and October, certifying his knowledge of various roads.

I was on night shift on Monday 29 August 1966 when the first of these Type 3 E.E. 1750hp main line locomotives became available for work at Thornton. It was of course secondhand, having been sent from Haymarket, the maintenance depot for the East Coast of Scotland. However, Thornton men had waited a long time to sample the comforts of main line diesels which promised to be so very different from the hard-up steam engines.

I had earmarked the Type 3 for the 1a.m. Conditional, a local trip train whose driver was familiar with that particular kind of locomotive; at least, that is what his route card indicated. The timing also suited the locomotive's return to shed early enough to undertake its next job, the availability being so greatly improved to that of a steam engine.

Dave Arnot and Dave McKinnon were the men rostered and I looked forward to seeing their reaction when they saw a Type 3 marked for the job. Unlike some drivers, Dave Arnot never made a fuss about anything and on hearing he was getting a diesel his fixed smile became slightly bigger but his talk remained quiet and limited. His mate on the other hand expressed his delight more forcibly and reacted as if he had won the Pools. I could well understand his great pleasure since I knew what it was to take duty just after midnight and be faced with preparing and firing a big, dirty Austerity. There was no comparison between such hard labour and the relaxing comfort of a diesel and Dave McKinnon was quick to realise that fact as he went on his way rejoicing. My last words to Dave Arnot were, "You've got a good engine there, Dave, so look after it."

At the end of my shift at 6a.m. Tuesday 30 August I went home and to bed, starting duty again that night at 10p.m. It was then I learned that the Type 3 I had told Dave Arnot to "look after" was smashed up and requiring main works repairs at Doncaster.

Half way through their shift, Arnot and McKinnon were bringing 36 wagons of coal up from Methil. The Leven Branch main line signal was passed at danger and, instead of continuing on the main line, the Type 3 with its train went into the carriage sidings where the drivers were preparing rail cars and cleaners were busy with their work. There was one almighty crash as the heavy train collided with the rail cars. The locomotive cab was staved in and disappeared against the engine room while d.m.u.s stood up on end. Various people were injured and shocked, and emergency services had to be called. Drivers lay trapped and bleeding and women screamed. Dave Arnot was the most seriously injured and after treatment in Kirkcaldy hospital he attended Edinburgh Royal Infirmary as an out-patient. Months later I met him hobbling up the Waverley steps on one of his regular visits to hospital.

His mate, Dave McKinnon, must have seen it all coming for, although badly shocked, he baled out and escaped uninjured. Magnus Matthewson, who was head shunter at Thornton Junction, had a remarkable escape – he was actually uncoupling the six-car set to make two three-car sets when the collision occurred. As the cars were pushed above him pieces of metal tore his clothing, but he finally escaped with just bruising and a cut eye.

There were two rail car drivers in hospital at Kirkcaldy that morning, Steve Barclay and Jim Sharp, and when Willie Young visited them they were in adjoining beds. Making light of the matter and in a bid to cheer up the injured men, Willie marched into the ward as if it was the enginemen's bothy. "C'mon you lot," he said, "are you going to lie there all day?"

With my experience I knew what was expected of me and I had no doubt I would soon be familiar with Thornton shed and the men. But what about the sub-depots? I wanted to know these places, so that when the men came on the phone with problems I would know what they were talking about. I was not alone in realising this shortcoming of mine, for the District Motive Power Superintendent's assistant, Mr. Cherry, was also aware that the knowledge of the areas I have mentioned would be helpful to me in my work. It was he who arranged for Chief Inspector James Mercer to take me on a tour of Fife.

This was not a bus tour but a marathon and could compare with any Army forced march. We visited Markinch, Methil, Kirkcaldy, and Burntisland (where I met the Controllers). We went to collieries at Dysart and Cardenden, visiting signalboxes and yards en route. Jim Mercer set a fast pace and kept well in the lead climbing embankments. We sometimes had a meal in a yard bothy or maybe a colliery canteen and, being well known, Jim never came away empty-handed. At Cardenden, we met Darky's wife, Jean, who was a clerk in the goods office. We had a long chat together and I had a chance to get my breath back. It seemed the irony of fate that Jim Mercer should retire and end his days severely crippled and in ill health.

In contrast to Willie Young's youthful vitality and regular displays of burning energy, his immediate superior George Shand appeared relaxed and self-satisfied. George stayed at his desk in the office and his placidity was an assurance for long life. Darky, on the other hand, was the real driving force on the shift and made all the decisions, deploying locomotives and men as he thought fit. At least, that's the way it seemed. One day, however, Darky had a difference of opinion with his shed engineman who usually allocated power without question from the supervisor. As they just could not agree on a particular marking of the engine board, a heated argument developed outside the running office. While the two were hard at it George emerged from the office and, brandishing a piece of chalk, walked between the squabblers to the engine board. "Pit that yin there and that yin there," he said as he marked two numbers on the board. As he disappeared back into the office Darky and his shed engineman stood speechless. The seemingly uninterested George had shown his authority and there was no more arguing.

George was a big man and easy to get on with. When I first knew him he had about three years to go to complete fifty-one years service on the railway and about the same as a member of the N.U.R. He had been at Dunfermline and Kittybrewster (Aberdeen) and his last fling at Thornton was an encore. George could make people laugh without conscious effort, so that a few seconds always elapsed before he joined in the joke. He was on duty one New Year's morning when driver Jock Nicol reported for work but was not expecting to get any. After exchanging pleasantries and wishing each other the compliments of the season, Jock left the running office and was about to pass into the bothy for a lie-down when George said on sudden reflection, "Here, Jock, you might take that engine to Eastfield," and he pointed to a B1 outside.

Jock Nicol was built like a tank, broad of shoulder and with reddish hair. His wide jowl hung loose and pale at the best of times but that morning his whole appearance expressed utter weariness. For a moment he eyed George disdainfully from the ground to his white hair then in scornful tones he said, "Get away, you horrible man, I take back everything I said about a happy New Year!"

On another occasion, the shedmaster was out one Sunday morning for special crane work and he sat on the office safe chatting to George and me. Out of the blue George said to the boss, "What time is the crane due off the shed?" "Eight o'clock," replied the boss. "Then", said George, "it's bloody high time you were away. That clock's slow." The boss slid off the safe and was out of that door like a shot.

George looked amazed at the man's reaction and I don't think he realised what he had said or what prompted him to say it. But the effect was good and the fact that the clock showed the correct time was immaterial – George had made the gaffer run and turning to me he said, "That's got rid of him!"

Looking back now it seemed unusual for George to walk round the shed but during my first week at Thornton he went for a walk with me one day and introduced me to the place. It was like a repeat of Willie Young's performance. As we passed the store door George checked that it was locked and made some remark about security. I was impressed by his keenness and I couldn't recall anyone at St. Margarets who bothered about security apart from a carriage & wagon watchman who patrolled the place at night. George Shand's interest that day must have been for my benefit because during the few years I knew him he seldom ventured farther than the drivers' bothy. George let Darky do all the worrying and running about and that suited them both. Sometimes, however, they got on each others nerves and Darky would put his coat on and threaten to go home and leave the lot to George, whom some people thought couldn't manage shed work because he had been desk-bound for so long. In between placid George and fiery Darky there was Tom Milne the quiet timekeeper (or foreman's assistant) on that shift. My time with those three was amicable but the day soon came for me to take up my own position on Dave Leitch's shift.

Dave was wee and bald, with high colour on his cheeks. It was his custom at the end of each shift to sit at his desk and wipe his face with a sweat cloth just as he would probably do as an engine driver. As he wiped his face his bare scalp also got the treatment. We got on well together from the start but I soon learned that before my arrival at Thornton, Dave's life at work was misery.

He was then second man to Jock Todd who was very close to Andrew Morrison, the timekeeper. These two would often 'gang up' against Dave and withhold information relative to the job. For instance, the Control would tell Jock Todd that a particular engine was on its way to Thornton and Dave Leitch would learn about this when he saw the engine coming on shed. Or maybe a train's load would be increased, necessitating the provision of a heavy engine. This information would be kept back until after Dave had the shed set then Jock Todd would tell him what was required and the wee man would have to shunt the shed and find a suitable engine. Such pettiness in grown men is difficult to understand but it was to be found in many places on the railway. Little wonder Dave Leitch developed a happier disposition when he took charge of the shift and had a change of mates. The relationship between him and Morrison, however, was bitter to the end.

Andrew Morrison had a lot of rein with Jock Todd and this allowed him to exercise authority far beyond his position. He was used to having things his own way and any stranger walking in would have thought he was the supervisor. I don't think he knew quite how to take me when I came on the scene but he wasn't long in finding out who gave the orders.

It was the practice at that time for rail car drivers to carry a leather satchel which contained the driving control handle, brake handle, A.W.S. key and ignition key. This bag and its contents were deposited in the running office after each shift. I remember one particular night Bob Masterton arrived on shed with a set of cars and I told him to leave the keys and I would take them to the running office after the cars had been disposed of.

Bob, or Rab, as he was sometimes called, was a droll character and said something about, "You'll get it from Morrison!" I just laughed at Bob's style and went on directing operations. After he had signed off duty he passed me again and from the side of his mouth he quietly murmured, "Morrison said you've no bloody right to take the keys off me," and smiling over his shoulder he disappeared into the night.

I, in turn, disappeared into the running office and pushed my face through the open window close to Andrew Morrison. "Look," I said, "don't you ever again tell a driver or anybody else what I'm supposed to do or not to do. I'm the gaffer here and don't you forget it." His face drained of what colour it had and his eyes widened behind the thick lens of his spectacles. I left him speechless as I went out into the shed again. When I returned to the office for a meal break it seemed Andrew was on his own and said nothing as Dave and I chatted in the usual way. But I never bear a grudge and I realised there was enmity enough between Andrew and Dave without me getting involved. Before the shift was over Andrew and I were quite friendly, he as the timekeeper and me as a supervisor. We got on well together ever afterwards . . .

Before long I had a working arrangement with Jim Bruce the shed engineman and right away he and others were aware of a reduced workload. This was not my primary object but it was the one thing appreciated by the men. Dave Leitch's attitude to the job had been very different and practically every engine that came on shed had to be turned to satisfy his 'slave master' instinct. I reasoned that the more engine movements there were the more chance there was of an accident – a collision or derailment. Because of the distance to the turntable the work was time-consuming. So, it became my practice to allocate engines for jobs according to the way they were turned when they came on shed – providing of course the engine was suitable for the work. Turning engines could not be completely avoided but I kept it to a minimum.

When the rail cars were on the move during the night it was more important than ever to avoid conflicting movements. In the event of collision or derailment a locomotive could quickly be replaced but rail cars were not so readily available. During my turn of duty I normally gave the latter my close attention and waited until they were stabled ready for coupling up before I partook of my meal. This was a course I would have followed without instruction because I was used to outdoor activity at St. Margarets and enjoyed being involved in the work physically rather than merely in a supervisory capacity. But early in my career at Thornton I was to learn a hard lesson with regard to rail car supervision and I discovered, too, that my supervisor colleagues were simply associates rather than true friends.

It was the practice at Thornton on a Saturday for the night shift supervisors to relieve the back shift men at 9p.m. so that the latter could get to the bar before closing time at 10p.m. This arrangement was widespread on the railway, though unofficial. A Saturday evening at Thornton was very quiet and it was after 10p.m. before there was any real activity. On one particular occasion Andrew Morrison was already away for his pint whilst Dave Leitch and I sat talking as we waited for our early relief. Being practically teetotal I would have been quite happy to work my full shift but I was not unsocial and went along with the existing arrangement.

As usual that night George Shand put in an appearance at a quarter to nine and Dave Leitch was ready for off. Darky was never one for early relief although he accepted the arrangement and enjoyed the privilege when he was back shift. He wanted the best of two worlds, to finish at 9p.m. on the backshift and start at 10p.m. on the night shift. "Just you go away with Dave Leitch," he used to say. "I'll be out later." So it was on the night in question I was further persuaded by George Shand who told me to go along with Dave. I thought no more about it and duly carried on down the road with my mate who caught a bus for Kirkcaldy while I travelled likewise in the opposite direction, going home to Glenrothes.

Next day I was on my way to the Sunday afternoon ambulance class session for further training in first aid work when I met our chief clerk, Jim Dempsey. "Did you hear about the rail car pile up last night, Charlie?" he asked. As he went into details I felt deeply dismayed and very worried indeed when I realised there had been an accident on my shift when I was unofficially absent. That week on the day shift I was given all the harrowing particulars and soon realised I was in trouble 'up to the neck'.

After my early departure that fateful Saturday a driver by the name of Ken Ross was detailed to fuel and stable a triple set of rail cars which arrived on shed about 9.30p.m. He and his mate duly proceeded with the cars along the 'Fat Wife' to the western extremity of the yard and the shunt spur. After the fireman had pulled the points, the cars were driven forward, supposedly in the direction of the fuel sidings. But both men had failed to observe that the blades were not correctly across with the result that a serious derailment occurred.

When Ken Ross reached the running office to report the mishap Darky was already there and news of the derailment just about put him through the roof. He immediately panicked and in agitated fashion threw his arms about shouting, "I'm having nothing to do with it. It's Meacher's shift!" Knowing Darky, that word 'nothing' would probably be substituted with something more profane and emphatic.

George Shand was debarred from taking helpful action by Darky's influence on him. Willie Young dominated the shift and had relieved George Shand of much of his responsibilities. I understood this situation and concluded that only Darky could have helped me that night. It would have been a simple matter to have recalled me from my home and allowed me to see the situation at first hand. But he was in a sudden state of unreasoning panic, and fearful of blame. I was left to hold the baby and a week later when I took duty at 2p.m. on the Monday I was called before the Superintendent, Mr. Luttrell.

On my way to Dormitory House I passed a Black Five derailed all wheels at the shed outlet points and I thought, "They can't blame me for that!" I had been instructed to rendezvous with the shedmaster Thomas F. McKay, who lived in a railway cottage near the district H.Q. and he met me as arranged. He was no stranger to the forked tongue of George Luttrell but he accepted the superintendent's verbal lashings as part of the job. Driver Willie Bell, on the other hand, in his capacity as Union representative, would most certainly not put up with ungentlemanly conduct and more than once had been known to walk out of George Luttrell's office when the latter became outrageous and thumped the desk. I had never seen this side of the man's character but I was soon to be a close witness. As we entered Dormitory House, Mr. McKay said, "Let me go in first to see what kind of mood he's in, then follow me in a few minutes." I waited outside for a reasonably short time then knocked firmly on the chief's office door before entering.

Mr. McKay and Mr. Luttrell were seated on the same side of the big desk where not long before I had been interviewed for the running foreman's job; as I sat down opposite them I was mindful of the changed circumstances of my visit.

Mr. Luttrell was asthmatic and hard of hearing which resulted in an uneven temperament. He was known to reprimand his secretary if the sunshine annoyed him and would call her in to pull the blind down. His ill health had created an ill nature and his utter weariness was mirrored in his face as I sat waiting.

When he started he spoke quietly and it seemed he hadn't the strength to fight the apparent hopelessness of the situation. The derailment and damage to the rail cars was bad enough but my absence at the time really goaded him. I offered no defence and wholly accepted the blame for everything. He became outraged and stood up, half bent to thump the table. "Damn it, man," he said, "I don't expect you to pull points but I want you to be there and see they are pulled properly. Do you realise that during the past three weeks damage to rail cars has cost us £26,000?" (Dundee and Leith Central had also had mishaps.) Mr. McKay by this time was cowering from the din and pretending fright, but the thumping went on. "Have you nothing to say for yourself, man?" "No, sir, I have no excuses to offer." These words from me seemed inaudible in the din and only lip reading would have made them significant to Mr. Luttrell. "Keep this up," he said, "and you won't be a b—— running foreman for long. Go on, get out of my sight!" That was me dismissed and thankfully I walked out into the fresh air – back to work in time to organise the crane and breakdown squad for rerailing the Black Five.

On reflection I could have argued with Mr. Luttrell and put forward the point that the traditional early relieving at Thornton had not been honoured by Darky and the same Darky was actually on the premises when the derailment occurred. All this didn't alter the fact that it was my shift and I should have been there. But I do not agree I should have been supervising men setting points half a mile away from the running office. It would have been impracticable as well as unnecessary for a supervisor to accompany responsible enginemen on their movements about the shed. The trouble was the driver responsible could often be irresponsible.

Driver Ken Ross came to Thornton from Galashiels on the day I started at 62A. Before that he had been at Helmsdale where the pace was far removed from the urgency associated with the industrial belt of Scotland. The first I heard about him seemed to indicate that Thornton had been landed with someone not quite ordinary.

It is the custom for a driver to be given the opportunity to learn roads when he first comes to a depot. This chance was afforded Ken Ross but instead of learning roads he made visits to his home in Galashiels. On the train one day he sat beside Mr. Cherry, the Assistant Superintendent, who was unknown to Ken. They entered into coversation and the story goes that the man from Helmsdale quietly told his travelling companion how he had outsmarted the shed foreman. "He thinks I'm learning roads but I'm on my way to Galashiels," said Ken.

Such happenings, true or imaginary, did not bother me, nor was I concerned when Kenneth smashed up a train of coal at Thornton Junction not long after he settled in Fife. My troubles with this driver were confined to the shed. He just could not not, or would not, leave the shed without finding fault with some part of the locomotive. With the demise of steam it was the simplest thing imaginable to fail an engine but most drivers ignored the deterioration. Not Ken. No sooner was he aboard than he was down again chasing foremen and fitters. I was so incensed with his delaying tactics after providing him with a good engine that I once booked him off and detailed another driver for the job. He went to a higher authority and was paid for his shift, I think, but I had made my point and Ken did not give me any bother after that.

The men at Thornton had various modes of transport to and from work to supplement the public bus service, which didn't cover the 24 hours. There were cars, motor bikes and push bikes whilst some used the trains, walking the mile or so from Thornton Junction station. Sometimes there was the chance of a lift on a goods train passing the shed.

This handy conveyance became available one morning when a goods train stopped directly opposite the shed on the Cowdenbeath branch line. It was routed via Thornton West and Thornton South to Kirkcaldy and a firedropper heading for home climbed up on the engine. On seeing him, the driver smiled and stepped aside and the firedropper accepted the unspoken invitation to take over the controls – after all, it wasn't every day a lowly paid labourer had the opportunity to drive a train on the main line.

Slowly, the goods train moved clear of the branch curvature at Thornton South and the pace quickened towards Dysart with clear signals all the way. At Sinclairtown the brakes were applied and the train ground to a halt at the station platform where the firedropper stepped down with a bright, "Cheerio! Thanks for the driving turn." "Here!" shouted the driver. "Where are you going?" Somewhat surprised, the firedropper stopped in his stride and, turning to face the driver, said, "I'm going home." "Going home!" said the driver. "Are you not conducting me to Iverkeithing?" At this the firedropper's mouth fell open and he could only shake his head in negative reply.

Being dressed in engineman's uniform, the firedropper had been quietly accepted as the conductor requested by the Glasgow driver who was returning home via Kirkcaldy instead of Cowdenbeath – the real conductor was still at Thornton shed and had to be rushed to Sinclairtown to get the train on its way . . .

Individuals with a peculiar characteristic were not confined to the Motive Power Department at Thornton. There was a signalman at Thornton Weighs who never answered the telephone. When called he would take the receiver off the hook and it was the click that told the caller he was through, but the caller had to talk first. This was an idiosyncracy of Willie Davidson, who had been in the Weighs signalbox for fifty years. At the beginning of his railway career he had been a signalman at St. Boswells for a short period but when he came to Thornton Weighs his stay there must qualify for the *Guinness Book of Records*.

I was in the box one day just after Willie had taken duty. We were talking about his long career at Thornton as his mate put on his coat preparing to go home. Willie stood close to the shining signal lever frame polishing a lever handle in the customary manner. "Yes," he said "fifty years in the one box takes some beating." Just then his mate made his exit and looking back over his shoulder he quietly said, "Aye, but you'll be longer in the next box!"

When the rail cars arrived on shed they were supposed to be empty and it was the guards responsibility to ensure they were and that the doors were properly secured. Some guards used to bale out at the approach to the shed to avoid a long walk back to the station and the cars would come in with only the driver aboard. And he, I may say, was ready to detrain as soon as the wheels stopped turning.

The last passenger train off the branch on a Saturday night came from Edinburgh and was rightly known as 'the boozer'. On one occasion when this train arrived on shed as 'empty coaches' I found a drunk miner aboard who should have alighted at Cowdenbeath. He was a big strong fellow whose hands were evidence that he had hewn a lot of coal in his time. He was not unruly but very drunk and a nuisance when there was work to be done. I had to be rid of him quick – but how? It was well after midnight and public transport had long ago ceased to run.

There was, however a main line diesel off repairs and waiting for a test run. I detailed two men to take this locomotive to Cowdenbeath and notified the Control accordingly. The miner, who by this time had filled his lungs with cold night air was near sober and he was despatched with the diesel. Before he left, however, he insisted on paying for the trip and with about four pennies in his hand kept saying, "How much am I due you, pal?"

These incidents with overcarried passengers reflected badly on guards and station staff, and on one occasion turned out to be a most serious business. I was back shift when the early cars came on shed just after 6p.m. The disposal men fuelled then stabled the cars and everything was going well. Johnny Ross was the fireman on the job – a very good worker and conscientious. The last sets of cars to arrive at that time in the evening were being fuelled and there were two sets in the shed. All seemed in order and I proceeded to mark the engine board to allocate steam engines for particular jobs. It was then Johnny Ross came to me and said, "Charlie, there's a toilet showing 'occupied' on that first set in the shed." "Well", I countered "go and see if there's anyone inside." I said this in jest because I considered Johnny had done his part by alerting me to the situation and, having finished with the engine board, I went to investigate.

The set of cars involved was in No.5 road, where they were examined and had engine sumps replenished prior to going into No.1 or No.2 road. Jock Foote was the fitter on the job and I told him to stand by in case he was required to take the door off. But first I tried a trick my father had told me about when he was on the trains and had similar trouble. This called for a piece of rubber, an eraser, for instance, and I had one in my dust coat pocket. I pressed the rubber hard against the white metal disc and forced it over to the right. As I worked Jock Foote was looking interestedly over my shoulder and no doubt learning something. Jokingly I said to him, "If there is a body in here I need room to get off my mark, so stand back a bit." I don't know what he thought I said but the next thing I knew Jock was at the other end of the coach watching from afar. "Come here," I called to him, "and give me a hand with this door."

My trick with the rubber had worked and the lock was free but I could feel an obstruction as I put pressure on the door. After more effort the door opened very slightly and on the floor I could see a head. I pushed my face close to the gap and glimpsed a man on his back with slashed wrists, his arms bent near his head.

My heart was pounding as I stood back and, controlling myself, I quickly said to Jock, "There's a man's body in there. I'll go and get help." Still managing to keep a grip of myself I returned to the running office and phoned for the police and ambulance, remembering to emphasise the Motive Power Shed because mistakes had been made before and the emergency services had gone to the New Marshalling Yard.

I then walked into the enginemen's bothy as if on a normal visit and, as usual, the men there fell silent with my approach. In level tones I told them what had happened and detailed a fireman to meet the ambulance and escort it across the rails and into the shed close to the rail cars. I remember after announcing my finding Jim Lawrie, a driver, swung his leg over the form he was sitting on and said, "Is that a fact, Charlie?" Nobody rushed to assist and it was with relief I saw driver Jock Stuart standing outside reading the notices. He was not on duty, this being apparent by his dress, but he was trained in ambulance work and a very willing person. I immediately explained the position to him and together we went to the rail cars.

There was some work involved in taking the toilet door off but eventually the tragedy was fully exposed. With the help of the ambulance attendants, we somehow manoeuvred the body out of the rail car and into the ambulance. The unconscious man still had a pulse and before long he was being rushed to hospital.

We later learned he survived an attempted suicide (overdose and slashed wrists) and after treatment at Kirkcaldy was removed to a mental hospital at Cupar.

George Hume, the station inspector, whose staff should have inspected the train and toilets was shattered when I broke the news to him. But it was Johnny Ross who was more deserving of praise for his keen alertness. Had he not observed and reported that 'Engaged' toilet, help would have been long delayed.

Help was long delayed on one other occasion in Edinburgh and a life that might have been saved turned out to be a fatality.

The evening train from Perth was booked to arrive at 9.29p.m. in No.19 platform at Waverley. It was always a rush to detrain passengers and unload mails before the empty coaches were hauled out to Saughton Carriage Sidings where they lay all night. In the morning they were brought back to Waverley to be cleaned prior to working the 10.3a.m. to Perth. One morning a man's dead body was found in the toilet and, who knows, had he been found the previous night he might have been alive and responded to treatment.

In the immediate post-war years the Railway Executive employed

975 people at Thornton, 700 at Dunfermline and 362 at Ladybank. Most of these were engaged in the Operating Department and Motive Power Department, with some permanent way men and workshop staff at Ladybank or elsewhere.

During my time at Thornton the transition from steam to diesel traction was under way and Beeching cuts plus staff cuts were the order of the day. It was my privilege and pleasure to know and work with the old school at Thornton as well as their younger colleagues. I remember well during a quiet period on the day shift I would sit up in the cab of the shed shunting engine, usually a J36, and listen to Ebenezer Reid as he related stories about days long past. Eb was a sentimentalist and tears would well in his eyes as he remembered the railways he loved. In his retirement I took him to the vacant spaces that once housed Thornton shed and he wept unashamed.

This pride and love of railways can be inherited and shared by succeeding generations and there are many examples of this. One had to be careful at Thornton because some people were interrelated and, being a stranger, I avoided open criticism of enginemen rather than possibly cause offence. There was no chance of adverse criticism when it came to the Lowe family, however.

The father, Dave, was a very dependable driver and running foreman. He was known affectionately as 'The Diver' because it was said he had once dropped his gold watch into the wet ash pit and he jumped in to retrieve it.

His son, Bert Lowe, was both friendly and industrious; had I been able to choose my team at Thornton I would have picked Bert and a half a dozen like him. Being such a good worker he experienced physical upset if anything went wrong. This distress overwhelmed him one day when the Austerity 2–8–0 he was driving became derailed at the west end of the shed.

Bert, like a captain on a sinking ship, stayed with his engine until the breakdown crane moved into position. Mr. McKay wasn't very well acquainted with Bert at that time nor Bert with the shedmaster, who was always amicable and easy to approach. As was usual, Mr. McKay questioned the driver as to how the locomotive became derailed and the friendly Yorkshireman used friendly Yorkshire phrases like, "Now, suun (son), tell mi wat 'appened" and "Y'alright, suun?" This gentle approach had the opposite effect to that expected and all the anguish and misery that Bert felt suddenly exploded. "Don't you suun me," he shouted at Mr. McKay. "You're no ma faither!" Such a tantrum was completely out of character, but understandable in the circumstances, coming from one who cared about the railway.

On the whole I got on very well with Mr. McKay and I soon learned to appreciate his sense of urgency when the breakdown crane was required. He just could not and would not tolerate any undue delay. There were always two B1s on standby at Thornton and it was customary to use one of these. However, steam had to be raised and the tank topped up before going on to the breakdown crane. This work was in the process of being done one day when Mr. McKay appeared rather quickly after being called out. I could see him coming towards me looking angry and he gesticulated towards the B1 which was throwing smoke to high heaven. There was no doubt what was making him angry but as soon as he came into hearing distance I parried an expected verbal volley with my own outburst. "Some of these men will be late for their own funeral," I said. "That engine should have been on the crane long ago." The shedmaster looked somewhat taken aback but his mood changed and his clenched fist shot forward in forceful gesture. "That's the stuff, Chas," he said. "Chase them up." Very often after that when we passed on the road and in the shed his greeting would be preceded by that piston-like movement of his fist . . .

Apart from our contact at work we also met at the Ambulance Class where we learned first aid. Ruben MacLean and George McCaig were two senior drivers who had given many years to this important service. They prepared the lecture hall and organised competitions, being always ready with advice. A doctor came from Kirkcaldy every Sunday during the session to instruct on treatment of various injuries as well as accident procedure. The business was not always serious – sometimes we had a good laugh.

I remember a very keen ambulanceman came from Ladybank to put us through our paces and he insisted on realism. To a learner, this isn't very easy, as I soon discovered. When my turn came for exercise the Ladybank man told me to imagine I was out walking in the woods with my girl friend when she fell on rough ground and punctured a varicose vein in her leg. "Now," he bellowed, "what would you do?"

I was conscious of a heavy silence and the class waiting for my reply. Slowly I began to explain about covering the bleeding area with a hand and pressing firmly until a suitable dressing or bandage was available. Put patient on her back and elevate the leg; then I stalled. "What else?" said the man from Ladybank. I just couldn't think 'what else'. Then in his broad Fife dialect he said, "Take off her suspender belt, man, and any other constricting clothing." That's how I learned to deal with a burst varicose vein and struggle with a girl's suspender belt . . .

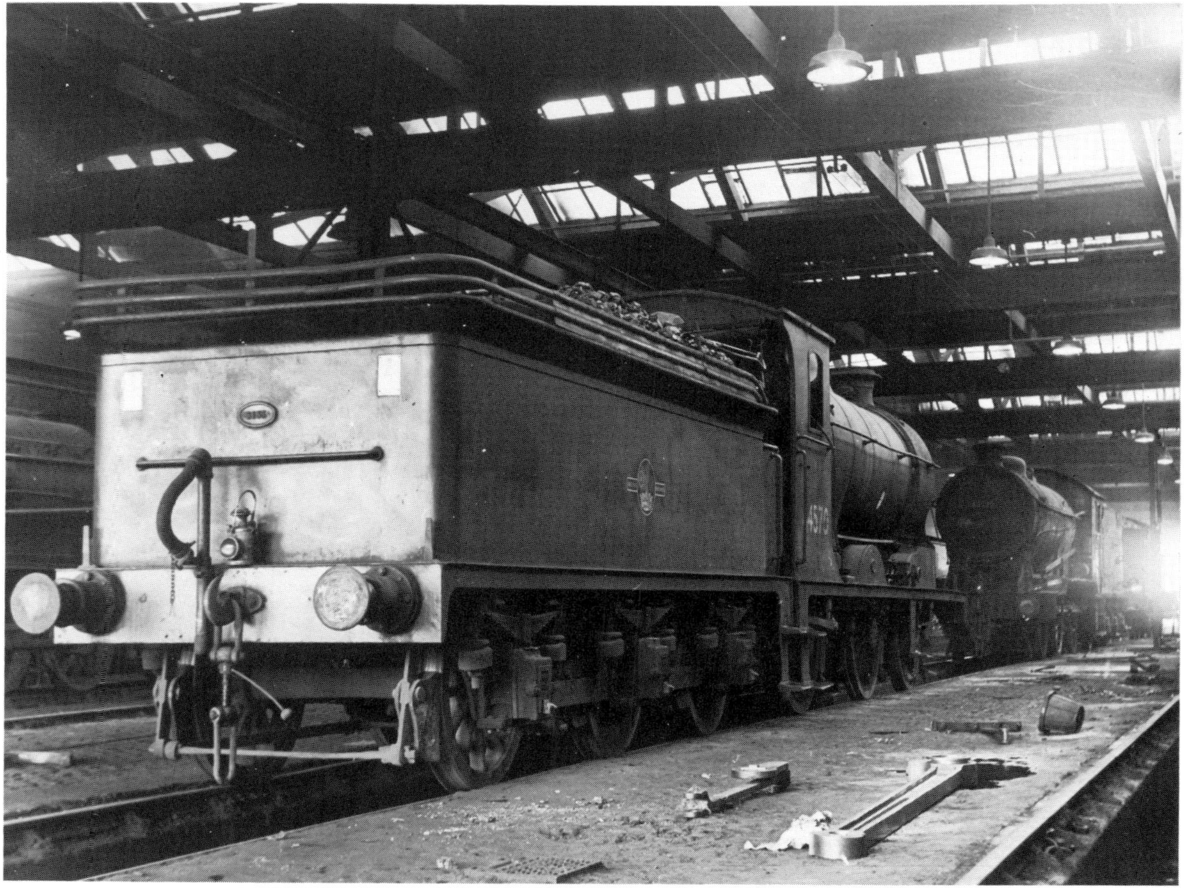

J37 No.64570 faces up to J38 No.65920 stopped for boiler washing and repairs in Number Five road at Thornton. Note engine parts and empty sand bucket lying together (what a combination!). Twin electric wires in roof supplied low voltage for portable lighting. [W. Laird]

Bob Barrie was a senior shunter at Thornton and a very keen ambulanceman. He was on duty on 1 March 1966 when Dave Taylor, a C. and W. oiler, was fatally injured by a train. This accident was the main topic at the next first aid class and I remember Bob saying, "We practise for years to deal with accidents and injuries and when the chance comes to put our training to the test the patient dies before we can make a move."

My ties with St. Margarets were not completely severed during my time at Thornton. Men from 64A very often came on shed at night and I was able to renew acquaintances. When they brought locomotive coal from Edinburgh they usually took the train direct to the coal sidings and after coupling off they either went to the New Yard for return working or left the engine at Thornton and went home passenger. The signalman at the Weighs used to advise the running foreman when this coal was 'on the doorstep'. On being advised one night I made my way towards the sidings to await the train's arrival.

In the shadows beyond the signalbox I saw the outline of a J38 and as it passed the spotlight on the wall of the box I could see it was hauling coal. But instead of going into the coal sidings the locomotive and train came to a stand below the coaling plant not far from the disposal lyes.

On looking up at the cab I recognised the familiar features of Jack McDairmid, otherwise known as 'Palsy', because of his friendly "Pal" greeting to everyone he came in contact with. Having worked with him for years I knew him well. He had been harum-scarum in his younger days and after being a prisoner of war for six years he enjoyed life to the full. It was when he married that his way of life changed and he became more settled, but he was still very easy going and somewhat carefree.

"Well, Pal," I said, "what brings you in here – are you pathfinding?". "Oh, hello, Charlie," said Palsy as recognition dawned and his face was a huge grin. He obviously didn't know where he was but if he didn't move quickly some Thornton man hurrying on to the disposal might collide with his rear end. "Just stand there a minute." I said, "and I'll get you a conductor." Having failed to go direct into the sidings it was now necessary to take the train to the west end and propel back from there. Palsy was relieved in more ways than one when Thornton men took over and disposed of the train.

George Dickson, another St. Margarets man, made a more serious blunder not far from the shed at Thornton. He was on a north-bound freight with a B1 and lost control on a falling gradient passing Dysart.

The Thornton South Home signal was passed at danger and the B1 went over the embankment when it became derailed at catchpoints. The enginemen managed to get clear but the B1 was a sad sight with underside exposed as it lay on its boiler. In his spare time George was a magician and entertained at parties and other gatherings but his magic did not help him that misty morning.

The time soon came for Dave Leitch to retire and I was sorry to see him go. His place was taken by Jimmy Ritchie who had come through the grades at Thornton to the position of Locomotive Inspector. It was Jim who had helped the Thornton men to master the intricacies of diesel traction and A.W.S. I had often seen him with his 'pupils' at Edinburgh putting them through their paces and there is no doubt they were well tutored.

Jim's hair was white and soft and his complexion very fresh. He was tall, erect and always smart in appearance. But most striking of all was his even temperament; never once did I see him roused in rage or even in a bad mood. Little wonder he was well suited as a Leader with the Railway Touring Club, a position he held for umpteen years. His international travels also widened his outlook and there was none of the parochialism inherent in some Fifers. Here was a man who could see beyond the boundaries of Kirkcaldy and he had an ear for people who spoke of distant parts. We also had a mutual friend in Jimmy Good, a St. Margarets driver who was housebound through ill health. So we were never short of conversation and the handsome Class 1 man enhanced the appearance of the running office while I performed elsewhere. When Jim was off on rest days and holidays I sat at the desk and Harry K. Brown, the relief foreman or, in his absence, a driver acting foreman would cover for me.

The desk job called for overall supervision, liaison with Control and writing in the Log Book. At St. Margarets the Log Book was used only for important matters and the information was usually a scrawl, while engines for boiler washing were marked against respective shifts at the foot of the page. It was all very different at Thornton where everything was detailed and neatly written with the senior shift foreman's name at the head of each chapter. So, there might be an entry as follows: Driver James Sharp and mate preparing engine 64569 and taking same to Markinch to change 64582 which has a hot big end; or, Driver William Mair and mate with engine 61308 taking fitters to station to attend rail cars working the 10.40a.m. ex Edinburgh – fan belt missing and engine sumps to fill.

This was all very informative and it would not have surprised me to see an entry reading, 'Passed Fireman Walter Jackson found sleeping on duty at 10.22a.m.,' but was it really necessary? The senior running foreman, D. H. Thomson, was a real scribe and his writing was perfection. Dave was the only supervisor who had graduated from the fitting shop, all others being footplate men. He came from Motherwell originally, but prior to coming to Thornton had been shedmaster at Oban. With his technical knowledge and ability he was able to hold a dialogue with the fitting staff and met Mr. McKay on equal terms. His tidy mind, however, revealed itself in his appearance and his neat handwriting to those who knew him less intimately. My contact with him was confined to changing shifts and I smile to recall his words one night when I relieved him at 10p.m.

We talked for a few minutes about past events and coming events and Dave was on his way out when, as an afterthought, he turned and said, "For goodness sake, Charlie, put something in that book." It was

A2 Pacific *Sayajirao* (No.60530) heads a fast freight on the 1 in 70 approach to the Forth Bridge. This was the locomotive involved in the Longniddry accident on 17 December 1953 and referred to on page 105 of my *L.N.E.R. Footplate Memories*. [Authors Collection]

more for devilment than anything else that I decided to leave my space in the book a blank. I reasoned that if a depot like St. Margarets could get by with possibly a single entry then Thornton could manage without a Log Book at all. But, really, log entries came easy to me and they were useful for keeping shifts in touch with each other. Instead of incurring unpaid overtime talking, as often happened at St. Margarets, it was possible at Thornton to change shifts in the passing with a brief nod and the phrase "It's all in the book."

For a while Dave Lowe (Bert's brother) and Jim Crawford were accommodated in the running office during the day from 9 to 5. These were the clerks responsible for the enginemen's rosters, which were watched very closely by the men and the Trade Union representative. Any wrong move on the clerk's part was soon brought to their notice and, inevitably, there were arguments.

One of Dave Lowe's last jobs for the day was to prepare a list of spare men for the forthcoming 24 hours starting at midnight. This list was put in a clip on the running foreman's desk so he could see at a glance how many men he had at his disposal. Sometimes there was a set of men every two hours, or there might be a single driver at a particular time and a fireman at another time. On occasions the sheet looked crowded but very often there were blank spaces. The Control was made aware of the manpower situation and the locomotive controller (Gordon Grant on my shift) might come on the phone and say "Hello, Charlie, have you anything in mind for your 6 o'clock men?" If I said I hadn't he might say, "Well, we're thinking of running a special if you have an engine to go with the men, but I'll confirm that in time to let you get organised."

This is an example of the close liaison between Control and the running shed and in my position as senior foreman on the shift I would tell my No.2 what to prepare for so he could organise his shed accordingly. Harry K. Brown was usually the man to be advised and I think it would be true to say Harry was popular with everyone. A Methil man, he was, like so many other Fifers, close to the kirk and a church elder. At his work he used up a lot of nervous energy; when physical and mental effort were not in demand Harry's excitable system was vented through endless chatter.

Unlike other supervisors he never gave men a direct order. The whole background of the operation in hand had to be explained, and any plan forming in his mind was translated into a rapid verbal flow. Most of the time he would be roaming the shed and conversing with fitters, firedroppers, permanent way men or anyone else who would listen, or pretend to listen, while he talked incessantly. It seemed he knew everybody intimately and everybody knew Harry K., as he was affectionately called. Even when he sat down for a meal he was agitated and his fingers would strum the table while his foot kept time in restless accompaniment. If one took advantage of Harry's temporary involvement with food instead of chatter and tried to have some say, his acknowledgement would be interjections of "Aye" in a detached sort of way. When he deputised for the senior shift foreman it seemed his character came to life in the pages of the log book and his scrawl was in marked contrast to the neat entries made by D. H. Thomson.

The running foreman's desk was in a corner facing the office door and there was a window to his right front and another behind him, the latter having a cramped outlook to the gable and entrance to the canteen. Immediately on the left of the desk there was a stove with unlimited supplies of locomotive coal, while filling the other corner was a large telephone cubicle with table and chair inside. There was a chair against the wooden wall of the cubicle and adjacent to the stove, this chair being reserved for the outside running foreman during his idle moments.

Next to the telephone cubicle – the upper part of which was constructed mostly of glass – there were two desks used by the roster clerks and situated below a large window looking out on to the back of the shed and a view of open spaces usually blocked by wagons. Behind these desks, in a corner, there were coat hooks, a wash hand basin and a broom cupboard. The timekeeper's alcove and booking-on window were at right angles to this in line with the entrance facing the running foreman's desk. Against the wall to the right front of the desk there was a long low cupboard for storing books and timetables and the top of this cupboard was used to stack weekly advices, etc. The drivers' rail-car satchels were suspended on hooks on that part of the wall between the door and the long cupboard. Squeezed in between the foreman's desk and the long cupboard was a heavy safe and here were deposited the weekly wages and salaries when drawn from the bank the day before pay day. On top of the safe and against the wall there was a tall railway clock – aged in appearance, but a very good timekeeper.

I was speaking on the phone one day and my eyes idly looked at the clock. As the sun reflected on its worn face, I could see the faint outline of lettering across the bottom centrepiece. When I finished with the phone I stood on the safe and looked closer at the faded inscription and soon I was able to decipher the words 'Caledonian Railway'. Exploring further, I looked inside the pendulum chamber and marked in a corner was the name 'Banknock'. This was a station on the old Kilsyth and Bonnybridge line and the clock I had thought was an inheritance from the N.B. was, in reality, an heirloom from our greatest rivals. After Thornton shed closed and motive power operations were transferred to the New Yard the clock was installed in the Yard Master's office, so it may still be marking time somewhere.

There was a key rack on the wall beside the foreman's desk and keys for other offices or buildings were kept here, including that for the supervisors' toilet, a reserved compartment at the end of the lavatory block behind the shed. The most interesting key was that for the general office and if one had a mind one could explore this place in the

B1 Class No.61221 *Sir Alexander Erskine-Hill* shares Thornton's twilight years with impressive dignity. This product of the N.B.L. Company displays the ultimate in modern steam traction – electric headlamps, A.W.S., self-cleaning smokebox, screw coupling, heater and vacuum bags. This ex-Haymarket engine exudes pedigree. [W. Laird]

stillness of night. Actually, there was nothing to explore but the shedmaster's domain had an inviting fascination for some people who hoped to uncover confidential information. There was no mystery about the place and on the night shift a man would be detailed to light the fires and have the place warm for the '9 o'clock start people'.

This was not the best time to encounter Mr. McKay, especially if he had a hangover. After looking in at his own place, he would visit the running office and pretend he was reading the log book and understanding it. Any problems imparted to him didn't seem to sink in and he was soon on his way to the fitting shop which was more in his line than 'supplying power to meet traffic requirements and supervision of staff'. The best time to meet Mr. McKay was after he had had a refreshment on payday. He was in good fettle then and able to cast off his many cares.

I went to his office one day to discuss the calibre of men employed on labouring. It was nearing 5 o'clock – finishing time – and Nancy Hutchinson, the typist, stood impatiently beside the boss as he laboriously signed letters. Nancy wanted to go home and she grimaced intolerantly in my direction at Mr. McKay's very slow signings. Eventually Nancy hastened with her letters from the office and I face the 'Dandy', as he was called, across his desk.

He seemed near to tears as he said, "You know, Charlie, it was my dearest wish to have a daughter just like Nancy, but it was not to be. There is just my wife, whom I cherish dearly. I also have a collection of railway relics which adorn my home but when I go some heartless sod will put that lot in the bucket . . . Now, what's all this about workshy labourers at Thornton?"

I couldn't blame the men I was complaining about because they were of low intelligence, although alert in other ways. I just wanted the boss to know that he couldn't expect results from the kind of material I had at my disposal. He let me have my say then leaned across the desk close to my face. "Chas," he said, "I didn't employ these people, I inherited them." Smiling at this response, I wished I was as thick-skinned and could find solace in the anaesthetic properties of Scotland's national drink. We left the office together and as we parted at the door he gave me a friendly shoulder hug and said, "Go to it, Chas, keep the wheels rolling."

CHAPTER IV

More about the Thornton staff – loco maintenance – visitors to the depot – 60532 'Blue Peter' – Thornton New Yard and its history – Tunnel Wull – Rosyth Dockyard – John Cameron and his A4

THERE WERE two Mechanical Foremen at Thornton, Andrew Dowie on the day shift and Jim Innes, constant night shift. Andrew ended up at Aberdeen after a stay at Haymarket and Jim Innes went to Dunfermline along with Jackie Paterson, Bert Young and Jimmy Hepburn who had been shift foreman fitters. Jim Innes, who originally came from Springburn in Glasgow, lives in retirement at Glenrothes, but he is not idle. I met him in a supermarket where he is employed marshalling trolleys. When he went for the job the store manager asked him about his former employment and Jim mentioned his umpteen years on the railway. "You're just the man I'm looking for," said the manager. "Away and play trains with these trolleys." Jim works hard at the job and earns his keep.

Surprisingly, George Greer, the leading fitter on my shift was not accommodated by B.R. when he became redundant so he found employment elsewhere. George was a friendly wee soul with a disposition and sensibility that created a fine balance between laughter and tears. I recall one occasion when he argued loudly with Dave Leitch in the shed. George became hysterical and, losing all control of himself, he thumped and kicked the tender and framing of an engine. His condition was alarming and, turning away, Dave Leitch murmured to me "That bloke should see a doctor."

I never saw George in such a state again and I came to like him and his enthusiasm for the job. There were times when his keenness interfered with his role as supervisor and some fitters played on this weakness, if weakness it was. Someone just had to say to George he was having trouble with a particular job and George would end up doing the work while the so-called fitter looked on.

I used to revel in visiting him in his wee office in the fitting shop and disturbing his peace with the cry "What about it then?" George would look over his glasses and say "Now, hud on there – jist a minute." Still on the offensive I would say, "Are these washout engines ready for kindling?" George's mouth would drop open in surprise and he would answer "Awe, for goodness sake, man, I've jist started, the same as you." Still pressing I would tell him to get himself organised and into action otherwise I wouldn't pester him again. When my meaning was realised he would start laughing and begin checking the various jobs carried out on the washout engines. If the work had been completed he would tell me the engine could be kindled or perhaps he would estimate the time when an engine would be ready and he would say, "You'll get the Superheater (J37) in half an hour." This class was always referred to as a 'Superheater' by Thornton men whereas St. Margarets men called the ubique J37 an 'S'. More than once George had an afterthought and surprised me with "That yin on the drop pit is ready for kindling."

The 'yin on the drop pit' could well be a magnificent Gresley A4 and one of the last of the breed. In 1965 these locomotives were called in as substitutes for diesels on the gruelling Glasgow to Aberdeen route and they ran to diesel timings. The days when they were kept in trim at Haymarket for the fast East Coast services had long since passed and it was as if the points leading to the scrap yard had been pulled and they were given a new lease on life. Their superb performance over the former L.M.S. route while in a state of disrepair speaks volumes for their designer and the adaptability of the steam locomotive generally. But it was inevitable that this harsh treatment of the aging A4s should take its toll and the forceful drive against the terrain of the Scottish Highlands resulted in many hot axle boxes. These had to be 'doctored' as quickly as possible and the spare capacity at Thornton was used for this purpose.

Unlike St. Margarets where the drop pit was built into No.6 shed road, the wheel drop – as it was called at Thornton – was adjacent to but isolated from the shed. The building housing the wheel drop at 62A was, in effect, a small machine shop, with lathes and drilling machines

One of the 'Director' class on the turntable at Thornton when it was manually operated. Note the 'pusher' behind lamp post and wooden slats to give him more foot grip. The Weighs signal box is in the background. [Brian Morrison]

Thornton marshalling yard – a view of the west end of the yard showing four of the six secondary retarders. Cowdenbeath branch main line is on extreme right. Rothes Colliery winding towers are clearly seen in the background and opposite, though less clear, is Thornton motive power depot.

and work benches plus a vice at each position. Built into the wall of this workhouse there was an N.B.R. drinking fountain of the kind commonly seen on stations in Scotland. The words 'Keep the pavement dry' were an ornamental part of the cast-iron fountain and a metal cup hung on a chain in proximity to this antique. It would have been a good souvenir of Thornton and I was saddened to see it lying shattered when the time came to demolish the shed.

The smokebox jaws, corridor tenders and buck-eye couplings of the A4s were novelties at Thornton although unimportant to the workings there. I sometimes had to demonstrate to the firedroppers the operation of the smokebox jaws, which were opened and closed by a handle carried in the locomotive cab. This was placed in a hole through the framing below the smokebox and engaged with a square-ended spindle which was turned according to requirements. Apart from this, the A4 to Thornton men was just another steam engine, albeit a very good example.

After an axle box was re-metalled and fitted again, an A4 would be hauled off the wheel drop and placed in an adjacent road outside and there it would be kindled. Being such a big boiler and with cold water, one could not expect steam in two hours or so. These giants had to be nursed for a whole shift or more. When in steam and ready for traffic, the A4 would be allocated to one of Thornton's slow Aberdeen goods and in this way it would return to its home depot, run in and ready for more punishment.

During the time an engine was waiting to have axle boxes re-metalled, it would stand outside the shed minus the affected wheels. This was the case with an A4 one Sunday when things were quiet. Willie Campbell was the shed driver and I told him to stand beside the A4 to have his photograph taken. There was a great void where the 6′8″ driving wheels should have been and I suggested Willie should try and cover this space with his body – and him only 5′ nothing! When the photograph was developed there was Willie standing in front of a great hole in the framing and little else to be seen of the A4.

With the demise of steam Thornton became a mecca for steam enthusiasts and parties came from all over the country. On their arrival at the shed the person in charge of the group would report to the running foreman who allocated someone to escort the party during its visit. I recall a Saturday afternoon when two busloads of eager engine spotters arrived. It was a London club and those men and boys stormed the shed with such intense zeal it was as if the invasion of Europe was being enacted without the weaponry.

They seemed to be everywhere and didn't wait to be conducted round the place in orderly fashion. I remonstrated with the party leader when I found him and explained that he would have to form the visitors into groups and be suitably escorted. He blew a whistle more than once and this had some little effect but many had already strayed far from the flock.

We, of course, had prior notice of the visit but I never expected such disorder. Eventually three groups were formed with escorts provided and I made it my business to watch some of the strays. Being a Saturday, the lyes were full of dead engines, none more so than the disposal lyes. I stood in the 'Fat Wife' and looked through the space below the smokebox of another engine. I climbed through the cab of the W.D. to get a closer look and there I found one of the visitors busily engaged in removing the depot number plate from the smokebox. I shouted and the thief was so surprised he nearly fell off the engine. When he did get down he ran all the way back to the bus and disappeared amongst his pals. After their departure I discovered numerous depot plates had been removed and I realised these so-called 'enthusiasts' came prepared to pilfer – even carrying small adjustable spanners and pliers for the purpose.

It sometimes happened that a stranger would be seen wandering round the shed area without having consulted the foreman. From the office window in the early evening I saw such a person near the disposal lyes. I casually walked across and asked him if he had a permit to visit. He was most apologetic and explained that he was without such permission. He had hurried from his home in Leslie to take a few photographs before the light faded and that was my first meeting with the friendly Verdun Anderson, paper merchant, renowned for his steam locomotive photography.

But the most determined engine spotter I ever encountered was about 15 years old and had cycled from Bradford, visiting engine sheds en route. He reached Thornton about 10.15p.m. just after I had taken duty and I explained to him visiting hours were restricted to daytime and one must have a permit. On hearing this, his anxious smile gave way to sadness and he looked very disappointed. I gathered he was touring Scotland the hard way and he seemed to have nothing apart from the clothes he stood up in – principally a grey polo neck jersey and slacks. I asked him where he slept at night – various places, apparently, including under hedges and in bus shelters. "What about food?" I asked. "Oh," he said, "I manage alright."

Looking at him there under the shed lighting I thought about my own boys tucked up in bed and it seemed that's where this Yorkshire lad should have been. It was difficult to understand, travelling miles to look at an engine number and score it off a list. Had they been interested in the mechanical side I could have understood, but just looking at numbers . . . it seemed crazy. But who was I to judge a person's mental condition? Suffice it to say I admired the lad's pluck and, though the hour was late, I detailed a cleaner to escort him round the shed. After seeing the engines he went to the cleaner's bothy for a feed and a well-earned rest before heading for Dunfermline.

Such kindness did not go unnoticed because on another occasion when a visitor asked for the running foreman, Driver Henry Johnstone, (now a supervisor in his own right) pointed to me and said, "That's him over there with the soft hat and the soft heart."

Apart from Thornton's own allocation of steam engines, veterans were staged there waiting to be scrapped. Name plates, makers' plates, and depot number plates were removed for depositing in the material store and these eventually were sold to the highest bidder by the Stores Controller located in Glasgow. I remember applying for the nameplate off the B1 *Chamois* and was asked to make an offer. I had no idea what to offer and left it at that but I realise now the purchase of that nameplate would have been a good investment.

The short-lived N.B.L. main line diesels replaced by the A4s between Glasgow and Aberdeen were also staged at Thornton waiting to be scrapped. Compared to the heavy metal in a steam engine, the diesels had limited scrap value. Unlike the fixed redundant assets which a buyer had to remove within a certain period after purchase, the locomotives were delivered to the scrap yards at B.R. expense.

After weeks of storage a movement order would come to the running office advising the foreman that a certain locomotive had been purchased by a particular scrap merchant, usually in the Glasgow area, and had to be delivered on a certain date. This was important because of limited space at the scrap yard and the need to even out the work for the labour force. So, it seemed every consideration was given to the buyer of a steam engine. The purchase of locomotives was, of course, open to offer but B.R. profit must have been restricted because of the costs involved in delivering locomotives to the scrap dealer.

For convenience and in order not to disrupt other traffic, dead engines were moved from Thornton to Glasgow in the early hours of the morning. A driver and fireman had to be provided to man the engine doing the hauling and a driver was required to caretake on the dead engine. There would be enhanced payment for night shift time, also possibly overtime, whilst in addition men had to be employed preparing the engines for the journey. There was also the loss of the hauling engines availability for other work to be considered.

Little wonder I got round to thinking that B.R. should form a subsidiary company and name it B.R. (Scrap) Ltd. Thornton would have made an ideal scrap yard with its breakdown crane lying idle for long periods together with redundant boilersmiths and fitters with experience in using burning equipment. The scrap could have been loaded into wagons and despatched to the furnaces by normal train services. The human element would have been better catered for and kept in employment.

A significant exception to the redundant steam engines destined for scrap was the A2 Pacific 60532 *Blue Peter*, which came to Thornton from the north where it had been labouring for years. The nameplates and other 'vulnerable' fittings were removed, to be stored away safely, and the hulk of *Blue Peter* lay in tragic solitude in the shadows of the equally sad, winding towers of Rothes Pit.

It seemed to me this once valiant steed was also destined for the knackery until, one Saturday afternoon when I was on duty, a gentleman with refined manner came to look her over. He was suitably clad for climbing into the firebox and elsewhere, and made a thorough examination of *Blue Peter*. Later he asked to use the phone and I heard him pass on a favourable report to someone at the other end of the line.

Weeks went past and the A2 Pacific, looking very forlorn, stood there still fully exposed to the elements. Then we received a movement order indicating that *Blue Peter* was to travel south; it was brought on shed and suitably prepared for the journey.

I was night shift when Driver James Liddle (now Inspector at Haymarket) came from Edinburgh with a 900hp Clayton Paxman diesel to haul *Blue Peter* away. Being a keen engineman like myself, Jim made sure the 'big one' was well prepared for its long journey and we hoisted a barrel of cylinder oil on to the back of the tender to keep her going for awhile. So, it was goodbye to *Blue Peter* which had for long shared the torment of a depot in decline; it left Fife marshalled between a diesel and a brakevan. To date, the story since then has not been much less sorrowful and *Blue Peter* is still out in the cold.

During my time at Thornton, the New Yard was already a white elephant and shared with Rothes Pit more than a geographical proximity – both were financial disasters. Occupying an area of approximately 65 acres, this ultra-modern marshalling yard cost in the region of one and a half million pounds. Its construction involved about 430,000 cubic yards of excavation and embankment, resembling the opencast mining operations at nearby Westfield. Some fifteen miles of sidings were laid. There were primary and secondary rail brake retarders, automatic speed control and pre-selection route setting of points actuated through electrical relays.

Construction of Thornton New Yard was the third and largest stage of marshalling yard development and modernisation embarked upon in Fife. The first project was the extension of the marshalling yard and modernisation of signalling at Kelty; the second was the provision of the sidings and running loops at Oakley. So, Fife had a small family of white elephants as its fortunes took a turn for the worst so far as B.R. was concerned.

Thornton New Yard was sited on the Dunfermline-Thornton route approximately two miles to the west of Thornton Junction and to the north side of the main line between its connection with the Kinglassie branch at Redford Junction and a point where the River Ore passes under the main line railway at Clunybridge. For railway operational purposes the site was an admirable one as its location in relation to the railway network in Fife facilitated direct acceptance and despatch of trains from and to all routes. Unfortunately, traffic declined seriously and with the rundown and eventual closure of Rothes Pit, an integral part of the scheme disappeared and along with it the anticipated traffic.

The 3,000 wagons expected to be dealt with daily never materialised. Six reception sidings with a hump-engine rounding line arranged in tandem with 35 through sorting sidings, each of which held 55 wagons – some 27 miles of track in all, were never used to capacity. There were facilities for wagon repair and a tranship platform, also a 70′ electrically-operated turntable.

Three new signal cabins were provided: one at Clunybridge, controlling access to the yard from the west, one located within the yard precincts controlling internal movements at the east end and movements into and from the Kinglassie branch and the supply of empty wagons to the Rothes Colliery. There was also a new main line cabin built to replace the one at Redford Junction and this controlled the lines from the east and departures in that direction. The Control Tower was another important feature of the New Yard and this housed the plant for operating the retarders and sorting sidings. There was also an Administration Block at the east end and five subsidiary buildings including yard inspectors offices, staff accommodation, and carriage and wagon workshop. All this was illuminated at night by simulated moonlight provided by mercury-vapour lamps 55′ above ground level.

I became acquainted with this superb layout when I was a driver working trains from and to Edinburgh. On one occasion, we had been released from our train on arrival and I waited with the engine while the guard went to enquire about return working. Unfortunately, there was an argument and the guard came back to the engine in an angry mood. He made a variety of unkind remarks about the inspector he had seen, casting doubt on the man's legitimate birth. But what a surprise that guard received when the same inspector's voice came over the Tannoy threatening to take the matter to a higher level. Unknown to the guard – and to me – the engine cab was directly in line with a transmitter designed for the use of trainmen and the inspector had heard every defamatory word on the two-way system.

While the fitters at Thornton existed, so did their idiosyncrasies. Willie Milne in his capacity as examiner was the brother of Tom the timekeeper and Willie, being single, lived with his mother. For obvious reasons an examiner had to be a qualified fitter. Although tapping wheels and other engine parts seemed preferable to fitting axle boxes and big ends, it was a responsible job as well as a lonely one and possibly for these reasons there were few volunteers. There was no competition for it, thus it was a case of 'once an examiner, always an examiner'. Nevertheless, the importance of the work afforded good status and, so far as the running foreman was concerned, an examiner was a key man in more ways than one, none more so than Willie Milne.

Willie was the type of person who feigned disinterest when work was suggested and if I told him there was an engine in the 'Snaker' (Light Tunnel) to examine he would probably say, "Away and get lost," or words to that effect. It was improbable I would have to tell him anything else because he consulted the engine board for numbers and entered same in a wee book. The Light Tunnel was far removed from the shed, however, and when an engine went in there prior to boiler washing, I usually told Willie it was there.

This was important because the examiner had to take a note of any steam jobs, that is, leaking joints and coupling nuts, etc. and these would be reported and repaired when the engine was stopped for washing out. Though things didn't seem harmonious a kind of rapport developed between Willie and I and every time I told him there was 'one in the tunnel' I expected, and always received, a rude rebuff. Minutes later I would see the lights flash on in the 'snake pit' and I knew Willie was on the job. Always when he was finished, he would seek me out and quietly say, "That yin's ready in the tunnel, Charlie." Probably because of Willie's pretentious dislike of tunnel work, I called him 'Tunnel Wull'.

Harry Reid stayed at Leslie and was often my travelling companion on the bus to work. Harry was friendly, enjoying a laugh, and his exultation by inarticulate sounds was distinctive. When on day work he was employed as a fitter on steam engines, whilst on night shift he dealt with rail cars, examining them and filling engine sumps. This was when the smile was wiped off his face and his Jekyll and Hyde character came to light.

Men employed on marshalling the rail cars very often fouled the pit boards and Harry required use of these boards to cross the pits with a bucket of oil in each hand. These boards should never have been fouled, but some fitters were prepared to walk round the cars rather than cause a fuss. Not so, Harry. The sight of his pathway being blocked used to drive him crazy and his loud rantings could be heard echoing throughout the shed. He would stand there and shout until a driver moved the rail-cars. It only needed someone to come and say, "Fitter wanted at the station, Harry," and that was him completely demoralised and on strike until his blood pressure dropped.

It is laid down that when rail car vehicles are coupled, the coupling must be put on first followed by the brake pipes, control air pipes and jumper cables. There being such a confined space between vehicles it sometimes happened that the coupling was raised last. On one occasion, and possibly more, the coupling was completely forgotten and the train went to Leven and back to Thornton Junction before it was known that the two triple sets were joined only by brake and control pipes. This is made possible by the fact that in suitable conditions the power from the rear motors is sufficiently strong enough to match the pace of the leading cars. Even on the rising gradient from Leven to Thornton Junction, when gravity would be expected to divide a train, the power from behind was able to keep the buffers closed up and prevent serious damage to brake pipes, control air pipes and jumper cables.

While rail cars dominated the passenger scene at Thornton, the top link men were still using steam engines. These were usually B1s, the workings including the Crail Papers and the Rosyth Dockyard workers' train. The former came from Edinburgh and was worked around the Fife Coast by Thornton men, while the 'Base', as the dockyard train was called, started from Dysart. There was also a workers' train from Edinburgh to Rosyth early every morning and, although normally worked by Haymarket; I came to be the driver one morning when St.

Margarets took over special working for the Fife holiday. Instead of leaving the coaches at Rosyth for return working at night as was usual, I had to take them to Thornton Junction and work a special train via Cowdenbeath, picking up at stations en route to Edinburgh.

I duly arrived with my workers' train at Rosyth Dockyard where the platforms had names associated with Edinburgh. My mate uncoupled the engine and I rounded the train and the egine was recoupled. On the way to Rosyth I had rounded the train at Inverkeithing and had arrived at Rosyth tender leading, but now it was chimney leading and I was all set for Thornton Junction. The signal came off immediately and, with the gentle opening of the steam regulator, the B1 I was driving moved off with the train. As usual I looked back to see the train was following in the proper manner and I was amazed to see heads

Thornton B1 No.61103 crossing the Leslie Viaduct in August 1962 en route to Markinch with freight train. Designed by Sir Thomas Bouch, this structure has outlasted his ill-fated Tay Bridge and is now a walk-way between Glenrothes and Leslie. [John Leng & Co.]

sticking out of the windows, with hands waving and much shouting. I immediately slammed on the brake and stopped with the coaches still on the platform. Then the doors opened and the excited workers detrained. It turned out that these men stayed on the train and played cards before starting work. That was alright when the coaches remained at Rosyth, but their game was literally up when I took their gaming house away to Thornton. Like me, the guard was unaware of the card players' 'trick' because whenever he worked the job he returned to Edinburgh on the engine and another guard worked the train at night.

Haymarket engine and men worked the first part of the Crail Papers as far as Thornton; then returned home light engine. Included in this part of their diagram was the delivery of fresh drinking water to Dalgett signalbox between Arberdour and Inverkeithing. So, from the fast glamour trains of the East Coast they were reduced to the primitive delivery of water, but no doubt they appreciated the relaxed pace.

George McCraig was in the top link at Thornton and his friendly gestures at the ambulance classes were also apparent at work. Knowing of my keen interest in railways, he brought me all sorts of souvenirs from the Fife Coast railway prior to its closure. The ultimate was reached when he arrived with a dirty, black cylinder which he thought looked like a foot warmer of the kind used before train heating was introduced. I took it to the store and started to clean it; eventually it became evident that one end was rounded glass and the other end, which had a handle, was metal and was hinged to the glass bowl. It was, in fact, a pot lamp of the kind placed in carriage roofs above each compartment before gas and electric lighting came into vogue. Terminal stations had a large stock of these lamps and after they were cleaned and trimmed and the oil cistern filled, a man known as a 'potter' used to walk along the carriage roofs and drop the lamps into recesses, where they rested on their strong brass rim. The glass bowl was the only part within the compartment and, as can be imagined, there was only feeble light. Occasionally oil used to leak on the passengers' knees, especially when the train was in motion. An interesting thing about the pot lamp is the crusie, or cistern. This is a circular tank about two inches deep and oil is gravity fed to a burner centrally position at the end of the angled delivery pipe. The wick is in a detachable holder. The burner on my lamp, marked N.B.R., has a brass plate round the top of the lamp reading 'L.N.E.R. Kilconquhar No.2', which seems to indicate that this lamp was used at the Fife Coast station of that name – pronounced 'Kinocker'. This souvenir is a reminder of my good friend

George McCaig.

While I was happy with my pot lamp, a Fife farmer with pots of money and a great ambition, purchased the Gresley A4 60009 *Union of South Africa*. John Cameron was a cheerful character whose grey hair belied his youthful vigour and boyish interest in trains. He was physically strong and this, plus his rosy cheeks, identified him as a son of the soil. Farming was his inheritance but railways, especially steam engines, were his love. Never have I seen such enthusiasm for the machines that many enginemen were glad to see the back of.

John's love affair with steam started at an early age and, while his father tried to interest him in farming, John ran off to nearby Anstruther engine shed at every opportunity. He was lucky to have an uncle, Cameron of Locheil, with a seat on the British Railways Board in Scotland and this influential contact was an 'open sesame' to privileges other enthusiasts only dreamed about. An important one was a pass which enabled John to enjoy an intimacy with the footplate that thrilled his whole being. This was long before he became the proud owner of 'No.9' and the time when I first knew him.

After a hard day on the farm he used to report to Thornton shed about 5p.m. dressed, in every detail, as a driver – hat, jacket, overalls, the lot. He was destined for a return trip to Dundee working freight with a B1 and, knowing how seriously John felt about his hobby, the driver booked for the job used to stand back and let him get on with it. So, we had the situation whereby this fresh-faced farmer, looking like an engine driver, would come into the running office and say, "What's on the job tonight, Charlie?" Entering into the spirit of his keenness, I would tell him the engine number and where to find it in the shed. The driver and fireman became mere passengers as John drove and fired that engine to and from Dundee; when he returned to Thornton about 2 o'clock in the morning there wasn't a happier person in all Fife and he was as black as a Fife miner. He always finished off the job by writing a few repairs, then it was off home in his fast car to Lochty and a cat nap before starting work on the farm.

When he first purchased the A4 it was brought to Thornton for storage and John has since told me that his strategy was to ensure respect for his engine by gaining favour with the running foremen. He achieved this by subtle inducement in the form of venison, sacks of potatoes and the odd bottle of whisky, Mr. McKay being more than a little partial to the last named. I was usually too late to partake of the venison, but I understand the running office looked rather like a butcher's shop on occasions.

'No.9' had a low mileage when John bought her, having been the last A4 of the valiant diesel substitutes to have a general repair at Doncaster. John was somewhat annoyed when he discovered the tender had been changed but he soon had that matter put right. I do remember being up in the cab on one occasion at Thornton and I rubbed clean a white number just above the handbrake and this read 60004 which, of course, was the number of *William Whitelaw*. Tenders were always being switched for some reason or other but John Cameron watched every move and made sure he got the tender he had paid for. The low mileage might have been the farmer's reason for choosing 'No.9' but there is another consideration – a more romantic one – for John's wife came from South Africa, and thereby hangs a tale.

During one of his footplate expeditions, John was with Dunfermline men and worked a passenger train to Edinburgh. On reaching Waverley station the Dunfermline men went for their 'piece' and John stayed on the engine. There he was, looking every part a driver and winning the admiration of less exalted people on the platform. Two of his admirers stopped to take a closer look at British Rail's new image and John found himself in conversation with two good-looking nurses from Edinburgh Infirmary. One of these girls later awakened in John an emotion which, until then, had been smothered in steam; he made a shunt in his heart and found room for a wife. Now, at Lochty, while he specialises in steam engines, his wife breeds prize bulls . . .

It was my pleasure to take John to Edinburgh one day and introduce him to Norman McKillop (Toram Beg), then happy in retirement since thrashing the A3 *Spearmint* for years. After a blether with Norman, we went to see Jim Paterson who was also enjoying a well-earned rest. While at Haymarket, Jim had been No.9s driver for twelve years and his souvenir was that engine's steam regulator handle, highly polished and with the number emblazoned in gold. This was a handier thing to keep than Norman's mounted nameplate from *Spearmint* which decorated the fireplace until Mrs . McKillop talked him into getting rid of it when he presented the nameplate to an engineering club in Edinburgh.

Willie Young and Bob Mitchell, a locomotive inspector from Edinburgh who had also been won over by John, were with us on our evening out and after visiting my old Haymarket friends, the four of us went for a drink in an ordinary public bar. John paid for the lot and while we were sitting supping our beer and talking about everything but railways our farmer friend quietly produced a *Weekly Advice*, a little booklet issued by B.R. detailing Engineers Operations, etc., and for the information of the company's servants only. He then started reading out loud about temporary speed restrictions and other dry matters. After a single round of drinks I thought we would be going home to Fife, but no, there was more to come for we had a meal together, then I was driven right to my door. Taking advantage of the opportunity, I asked John to come into the house and autograph a coloured picture of 'No.9' for me, which he did with pleasure.

Back at Thornton the big A4 was being made ready for the road and the day came when a trial run to Dundee was arranged. B.R. enginemen were in charge but John was also there looking every inch a driver. At Dundee the engine went on the turntable before heading back to Thornton, and as the elegant sister of *Mallard* slewed round John Cameron stood enraptured and brimful of pride. Just then a local man spoke, disturbing John's ecstasy. "They tell me some wealthy Fife farmer bought this thing," he said. "Oh, is that so?" replied John, whose engineman's garb and grubby appearance disguised his identity. "Aye," continued the local man, "he wants his head looked," an aside that made the wealthy Fife farmer smile.

'No.9' did look a little out of place on the farm at Lochty but it now rests in the shadow of Haig's Whisky Bond at Markinch ready and willing to haul railway enthusiasts to Aberdeen or elsewhere. I last saw the 'maestro' at an open day at St. Rollox, and in the smell of hot oil from that magnificent A4 I re-lived in one joyous moment a lifetime with steam.

CHAPTER V

An accident in 1962 and its sequel – accident inquiries and reports – the No.1 Form – accident prevention – trouble with diesel shunters – reminiscences of Thornton Games and local personalities – subsidence in the area – pitfall posts – old enginemen's memories – the Fife coal trains – the Burntisland disaster – tests on the Forth Bridge – loco trials and increasing loads – drivers' memories – looking back

ALTHOUGH THE Tay Bridge disaster may have been the first and the worst railway accident in our area, it was certainly not the last. On 28 May 1962, for example, a steam-hauled train carrying 500-or-so Sunday school picnickers and parents emerged from the tunnel at Wormit, derailed and piled up in a tangled heap with the loss of three lives.

Exactly six years later, to the day, as a six-coach diesel train was on its way from Tayport to Dundee with about 80 passengers, the leading coach left the tunnel at the same spot immediately to the east of Wormit station. It had been caught by the set of points which served to protect the main line crossing the Tay Bridge 200 yards ahead. The first bogie of the leading coach held the rails on the sharp turn but the wheels of the second bogie jumped the line and scored along the track.

Two coaches were clear of the tunnel when the train stopped. Mercifully, no one was injured and the whole train remained upright. Railway staff went into the tunnel, helped passengers down from the four coaches there and guided them to safety. It seems the date '28' is unlucky for Wormit and the Tay Bridge.

It is important to establish the cause of an accident as quickly as possible and this is where locomotive and operating inspectors play a prominent part. They chase up the personnel involved to obtain their evidence of the situation. Where more than one department is concerned it may be necessary to hold a joint inquiry. If, for instance, a defective brake is the cause of an accident this could implicate the Operating Department, as well as the Chief Mechanical & Electrical Engineer's Department. Likewise, if the permanent way was suspect, the Chief Civil Engineer's Department would participate. Since it is overall an operating matter, the inquiry would be convened by that department.

Such inquiries are everyday affairs on British Railways and there is a laid-down procedure for conducting them. This is designed to disclose every applicable fact so that when the inquiry report is finalised the circumstances of the accident are readily apparent.

In the case of more serious accidents involving passenger trains, the inquiry is dealt with at Headquarters where there is a section of the Chief Operating Manager's Department fully employed dealing with accidents and irregularities of all kinds. Local managers are advised regarding who will be required to attend an Inquiry and arrangements must be made to release these people from duty. When they report at Headquarters they are called before the Inquiry panel consisting of senior officers from the appropriate departments.

In the Inquiry room there are microphones positioned round the table for the use of individual officers and witnesses whose spoken words are relayed to audio-typists in the same room. These girls are chosen for their typing ability and evidence is typed, word perfect, on three copies. After perusal, these copies are signed by each witness, one being retained by him.

The evidence is arranged in question and answer form and this information, duly signed, is put along with a summary of the circumstances of the accident compiled by the inquiry convener. There are also appendices which include information such as names and addresses of people injured, damage to rolling stock, permanent way etc. After all the evidence, the panel must then reach a conclusion, determine the cause of accident, and apportion the blame.

The Department of Transport Railway Inspectorate in London will probably have learned of the more serious accidents through the press or radio and television. Nevertheless, a report of the circumstances would be sent to this government department as quickly as possible, for arrangements to be made in the setting up of a Department of Transport Inquiry. To help the Railway Inspectorate in London to assess the circumstances and read the evidence available, a copy of the British Railways domestic report is sent to the Department of Transport.

Ex-officers of the Royal Engineers whose experience make them ideally suited for the job form the Railway Inspectorate. Working closely with them are the Railway Employment Inspectors who are recruited from the ranks of mechanically trained men with knowledge of railways – plus an inquiring mind. In some ways they may be likened to the Factory Inspectorate. So it will be seen that railway accidents are well documented and although domestic reports are restricted, the Department of Transport publish their reports through Her Majesty's Stationery Office.

As can be appreciated minor accidents and incidents inevitably happen all the time on the still extremely extensive network of Britain's railways and these are reportable in monthly bulk returns to the Department of Transport. Suicidal people, for example, recognise a train as a quick way to end their mental torment; derailments in yards and elsewhere are commonplace and on the whole occur without injury to personnel but, too often railway workers are injured or killed, usually because of a disregard of their own personal safety. When train drivers slip up and pass a signal at danger, they have committed the ultimate offence and are appropriately dealt with. This is where the locomotive inspector plays an important part.

This individual has to interview the driver personally and submit a report to Headquarters on the appropriate form. A driver with any self-respect is usually ashamed of his negligence – and honest about it. There could be various explanations for his lapse, including bad sighting of signal or bad rail, ineffective brake or bad judgement. The fact remains, however, that he has committed a serious offence and as if to emphasise the enormity of this breach of rule the driver is challenged by the signalman at the time a signal is passed at danger. Very rarely does the driver deny the signalman's accusation, especially nowadays when sophisticated signalling equipment can prove conclusively whether the signal was or was not passed at danger.

After obtaining all the details, the inspectors report is submitted to his immediate superior who passes it to Headquarters with a covering letter and any relevant witnesses statements. The report eventually comes before the Traction Officer who invariably recommends discipline. A charge against the driver is then drafted, and a No.1 Form is prepared by the Chief Personnel Officer for issue to the offender.

The form must be handed to the driver after the completion of a turn of duty. This is important because such tidings can cause trouble and adversely affect a man's work performance. The serious accident with the Aberdonian night sleeper train at Morpeth on 7 May 1969 is evidence of such a possibility. The Gateshead driver had been given a letter about late running on a previous trip and when he came to reduce speed to 40m.p.h. for the curve at Morpeth he failed to act quickly enough because he had been thinking about the letter. As a result the train became seriously derailed while doing 80m.p.h. and divided into five parts with the 'Deltic' locomotive ahead and on its own. Five passengers and a travelling ticket collector were killed, plus 121 passengers injured. This is why it is important that No.1 Forms should be retained until a man finishes his turn of duty.

If the driver accepts the charge he is punished accordingly and this is entered on his history card. A close succession of charges usually affects the degree of punishment, progressing from a severe reprimand to one or two days' suspension. After a period of about five years free from trouble a man being charged may benefit from his recent good record and be less severely dealt with. If he wishes to appeal against a charge this is heard by an officer who has not previously been involved. Like appeals in other places the punishment may be reduced or increased. On the whole, British Railways is very tolerant and an individual has to be a really bad egg before he is thrown out.

Accident prevention is a more worthwhile endeavour than accident reporting and all kinds of devices have been adopted by the authorities to avoid less dependence on the human element. On modern locomotives there are such things as automatic fire extinguishers, A.W.S. equipment to give visual and audio indication of signal settings, and the better-known Deadman's Safety Device (D.S.D.) or more simply, the 'Deadman'.

This safety device was very often abused by drivers who might isolate it for their own benefit. If, for any reason, it was truly defective then a main line train would require double manning. But wee Willie Campbell of Thornton was not on a main line train, he was on a diesel shunter alone at Markinch. The 'deadman' on this locomotive was a footpedal, one on either side of the box panel – allowing for driving from each side of the cab. It could be a monotonous strain keeping this pedal continually depressed, so it was not unknown for drivers to put a wooden key or similar item between the depressed pedal and the cab structure, thus effectively isolating the Deadman.

This was the position one day when Willie was concentrating on shunting Haig's Whisky sidings at Markinch. He was completely unaware of the approach of Inspector James Mercer who ascended to the cab on Willie's blind side. There he was caught red-handed violating a most important regulation and Willie was later suitably dealt with through the disciplinary procedure. But, in charging Willie, the inspector not only became unpopular with the wee driver, he also found himself in trouble with Willie's two sons who were employed at Thornton and were very close to their father. But such unpopularity is all part of supervisory work and, as President Truman once said, "If you can't stand the heat in the kitchen, then stay out," or words similar.

Jim Mercer was a good inspector as well as a dedicated railwayman and I remember when he was investigating a case involving an English Electric 350hp shunter which had been run at excessive speed to Ladybank resulting in serious damage to its traction motors.

Dave Maxwell was the driver and it occurred on a Sunday morning. It so happened I had hitched a lift on this diesel to Balgonie Bridge near Glenrothes, being on my way home off the night shift. When Jim Mercer heard about this he came to me and asked if the driver had exceeded the 20m.p.h. laid down. I was not aware of Dave Maxwell having done so, possibly because the stretch of track I had travelled over did not lend itself to fast travel and I explained this to Jim. He seemed satisfied and was just turning away when, as an afterthought, he asked, "Did you have a footplate pass?" No, I did not have a footplate pass and if ever again I was faced with the choice of walking three miles to my home or getting a lift to Balgonie Bridge I must say I would choose rail transport with or without Mr. Mercer's permission . . .

Although Jim was alert to rules and regulations and was on top of his job, there was a shyness about him that blunted his authority. This came to light one day when he visited the shed to interview a driver. He asked me if the driver was available and I told him his man was in the bothy. But Jim could not face the crowded bothy and asked me to tell the driver he was required outside. All he had to do was to open the door and call out a name but somehow he was reluctant to be in the limelight. Yet the same Jim Mercer was the founder of and driving force behind the Thornton Mutual Improvement Class which helped enginemen through the lines of promotion. He it was who devoted his spare time and energy to tutoring the budding drivers and the models he used to demonstrate his lessons eventually went to Kirkcaldy museum.

The incident with the 350hp shunting diesel and the burnt-out traction motors reminds me of more serious damage involving this type of locomotive. Instructions were received to transfer two 350s from Thornton to Stratford and these had to travel by the ordinary freight service. The two six-coupled locomotives were duly prepared by fitters, with the siderods removed and placed in the cab. This allowed the wheels free movement and made them acceptable for conveyance with other traffic.

It is a long way from Fife to Stratford in east London, and longer still when the journey is in slow stages. It was the middle of winter and one can imagine the low priority given to two dead locomotives, lying for long period in sidings en route. It seemed the two locomotives had been gone for months and they were completely forgotten at Thornton. So, it came as a shock when we learned that they had reached Stratford with their engines damaged beyond repair; the engine cooling system had not been drained and the extremely low temperature had caused a deep freeze and serious damage to the engines.

The great days of Thornton live on in the memories of many people, although so many more are, like their memories, beyond recall. Only the existing main lines and junctions give guidance to where once stood a very busy station. Apart from the daily hustle of an important railway station, once every year Thornton Junction used to burst at the seams. This was on the Friday of the Fair Week when Thornton Games were held, attracting a crowd of 50,000 or more. On that day specials galore steamed into Thornton 'frae a' the airts'. People came from Glasgow and Dundee. Prize money was over £200 at the beginning of the century – high winnings for the men who competed. And there was only one way to reach Thornton then – by rail!

Extra platforms were erected at the station for that day to cater for the thousands who streamed over the railway bridge and down Station Road on their way to the games. Willie Bell, the Union representative, who sometimes threatened to walk out on Mr. Lutterell's tantrums, remembered those days. As well as being a Union official, Willie was also a Games official.

In his reminiscences Willie would speak about those 'good old days' when, during the Fife holidays, he worked trains from Leven to Balloch on Loch Lomond. Each was absolutely packed, and at 2s.6d. return the outing was good value. While the trippers enjoyed a sail on the loch, trains went empty to Helensburgh to be turned. The passengers got back to Leven about 10p.m. tired but happy. Another favourite run was from Cardenden to Portobello for a shilling return and there was a choice of seabathing or indoor baths.

Burntisland Highland Games was a further attraction. Apart from conventional trains, 'Camel' steam coaches ran between Thornton and Methil. One of them, named *Brig of Don*, had a trailer coach for conveying children to school as well as for the Saturday afternoon and evening crowds.

Sir George Sharp is undoubtedly Thornton's most illustrious villager. His father worked on the railway from 1919 to 1946 and his brother James was an engine driver. Sir George had the same humble beginnings but was destined for rather more glory. He was, in fact, a driver at Thornton until shortly before I arrived there. I never knew him as a railwayman but I have met him socially and his after-dinner speeches are a joy to hear.

Thornton Class J37 No.64569 specially cleaned for a last run on the Fife Coast prior to closure in 1965. In the foreground, left to right: George Shand, Jock Traill, Jim Sharp, Willie (Darkie) Young, Alex Slimmings, Alex Wishart. In the cab Billy Hunter and David Laing. [Alex Wishart]

George was active in politics and for years was returned unopposed as Thornton's representative on Fife County Council. He joined the railway in 1935 and became a driver in 1948, a job he held for thirteen years. When he resigned his position at Thornton, he became commercial manager with a building firm and he went on to become Convenor of Scottish Burgh Councils. He was knighted in 1978 and is now chairman of the Glenrothes Development Corporation.

Sir George still lives in Thornton and chuckles at the memory of a new 'caller-out' who was sent to Thornton village years ago to knock up men urgently needed to work the breakdown crane. The new man dashed up to the village in the middle of the night. All went well at first. Then he came to a door where there wasn't the usual swift response to his knocking. He persisted and eventually a sleepy figure emerged. As the householder stood beside the half opened door the wakener shouted to him, "You've to turn out, all speed," then dashed off to waken someone else. The man he left behind looked mystified. The 'caller-out' had mistaken houses; instead of knocking up a railwayman, he had been thumping on the door of the local minister!

Unfortunately for Thornton Junction it stood above valuable coal. The coal company wanted £96,000 for leaving this intact – a sum which the railway company either could not, or would not, pay. The decision cost the railway years of worry. The Colliery company removed the coal beneath the station and the latter gradually began to subside. The platforms were built up as the station sank and just before Thornton Junction closed the paving of 1910 was below rail level! Ultimately the station had been built up at least 14 or 15 feet. The coal was worked from the old Balgonie Pit which was only 75 fathoms deep and it was said miners were so near the surface they could judge the time from the rumblings of a particular train passing overhead.

Because of the subsidence the original heavily-constructed buildings were replaced by lighter ones. Eventually the refreshment rooms were abandoned, as was a fruit stall which stood at the east end of the platform. Heavy cranes were also unable to work in the area.

At one time there was a gang of men whose constant duty was to ballast the rails to the correct level, since on occasions they sank appreciably overnight. It was about 1956 when railwaymen reckoned the subsidence had almost ceased. Where railways pass through coal mining areas, ballast has to be tipped to keep the railways safe for traffic. The reason for this is that when a seam of coal has been worked out, the pit props, which were put in to keep the roof up, are removed and the ground above gradually subsides, undermining the surface buildings and railways, etc., which sink with it. Structures will often lean at crazy angles and they may later have to be rebuilt.

During the time the subsidence is taking place the rails have to be kept up to a level that is safe for traffic. This is done by tipping ballast and lifting the sleepers on to it. Ash ballast was usually used at Thornton because it was cheap and easily obtained. Unlike the selfish coal owners in the past, part of the cost of tipping was recovered from the National Coal Board and the amount of ballast tipped was measured by 'pitfall posts'. They were made of concrete or wood and were placed at regular intervals of two chains (132 feet) alongside the track. The height was marked off on them in feet and the depth of ballast used to lift the rail to a safe level could be found from the pitfall post. This depth multiplied by the width and length gave the quantity of ballast used in lifting the track.

When I was at Thornton shed I never experienced any sinking feeling but the local permanent way ganger Dave Lowe must have had a greater awareness of the situation. While crossing the front of the shed one day with Dave Leitch we found the permanent way boss hammering in wooden pitfall posts adjacent to the tracks and close to the walkway. Being an ambulance man, Dave Leitch was always mindful of people's safety and he remonstrated with Dave Lowe about the posts he was hammering into the ground.

"Ye canna pit them in there," said Dave Leitch, "somebody'll trip ower them."

"Where else can I pit them?" asked the p'way gaffer. "I could tell you fine if I had a mind to," said Dave Leitch, "but what I am telling you is yer no pitting they sticks there!"

The placid Dave Lowe looked dumbfounded and was faced with a problem he had not bargained for. He wasn't the type to argue with anybody and certainly not with the Running Foreman who was adamant about the dangerous positioning of the posts. As we walked on Dave Lowe quietly began uprooting the posts and no more was said about the matter. Some time later when we looked from the office window we saw Dave Lowe nailing his posts to the ever-open shed doors – an ideal place for them. They were near enough the track to serve their purpose and would harm no one.

Over the years Dave Lowe and his squad won many awards for the 'best kept lengths' and these adorned the p'way bothy near the shed. I went in to see him one day when he was doing paper work relative to a bonus scheme and I commented on the numerous framed certificates.

"Those would make nice souvenirs for me," I said. Dave barely glanced up from his writing and replied, "You can take the bloody lot for all I care." I stripped the walls in record time and went home with a load of framed certificates for 'the best kept length'. I kept them at home for a long time before donating them to the Scottish Railway Preservation Society at Falkirk, where they will be more widely admired.

Ralph Barclay at 86 was the third oldest man in his native Thornton and could remember the Forth Bridge being opened on 4 March 1890 whereupon Thornton Junction became a vital part of the railway on the east coast. The first goods train from Thornton Junction to Leith Walk via the great new bridge was worked by engine No. 413, with driver Peter Cunningham and fireman David Graham.

For many years after the inception of the railways, Burntisland had been the hub of the rail system in Fife. Repair and maintenance work, plus the servicing of locomotives, had all been carried out at the Roundhouse, the fortress-like structure which was the engine shed at Burntisland. But year by year, Thornton gained in importance and in 1894 an engine shed was built on the west side of the main line at Thornton Junction.

As a boy of twelve Ralph Barclay was playing football with some other lads when he was told men in the wagon repair shop needed a messenger. For the next two years he spent his time running up and down to the village with messages or getting tobacco or other items the men wanted. His pay – sixpence a week.

One day during the Second World War Ralph was working the 2.50p.m. from Dundee to Edinburgh. When they reached Dalgety, an air raid was in progress and Ralph wanted to know what the position was. The signalman only opened his window long enough to shout, "I'm not coming out there to be killed," then banged it shut and returned to what he thought was a safer position behind all the glass.

Ralph didn't know what to do, so he continued towards the Forth Bridge. He wasn't exactly comforted farther along the track to see a gang of surfacemen sheltering under a bridge. He had a bird's eye view of the air raid and was glad to see the German planes head for home before the train reached the great spans across the River Forth.

Ralph liked to look back on the days when he could purchase a packet of twenty cigarettes for 5½d., whilst a pint of beer cost 1½d. – with a clay pipe thrown in free as discount. The drivers used to smoke these pipes until they were black and seasoned, carrying them in the snout of their bonnets. The pipes with small shanks were called 'jaw warmers'.

Those were the days of the great herring fleet at Aberdeen. Coal trains ran there every day and in turn the fish trains back were a daily feature, plying from Aberdeen all over the country.

James Jamieson was much younger than Ralph Barclay, but Jim could recall when, in 1920, he stayed at Ladybank and cycled every day a round trip of 18 miles to and from work at Thornton. Nobody thought anything about such a trip and some men travelled much farther, in all kinds of weather. In winter there were many occasions when they could only progress by carrying their cycles chest high through snowdrifts, so it must have been a relief when Jim moved to Thornton near his work.

On one shift he left his home at 7.30a.m. on Sunday and didn't get home again until 10.30a.m. next day. On the homeward journey on Monday it seemed the sixty mile trip from Glasgow was made by being shunted from siding to siding. They left Glasgow at 2.30a.m. and didn't arrive at Thornton until 10.30a.m. That was in wartime but meant he had been over 25 hours on the footplate.

At its peak, five lines radiated from Thornton Junction, going to Kirkcaldy, Methil, the Fife Coast, Dundee and Dunfermline. Even in 1956, every day except Saturday saw 60 passenger trains travel between Kirkcaldy and Dundee. This number was increased to 84 on Saturdays in summer. In addition there were 25 passenger trains a day terminating at Thornton and another 20 leaving the junction on the Fife coast and Dunfermline routes. Forty-three freight trains also passed through Thornton, whilst five more than this started or terminated in the yards there.

To recapture the real atmosphere at Thornton one has to go back to 1912, when the Fife Coast Express ran from Crail to Queen Street, Glasgow, in one hour forty-seven minutes. A first class return was 13s.6d. and a third class return 7s.6d.

Not many men in my time at Thornton could go back to 1912 and re-live the years when railways were at their peak. John Allan was a rare exception. He was verging on ninety when I first met him and, apart from a distinguished railway career, he had also been Lord Provost of Dunfermline at one time.

In 1906 when he qualified as a driver the wages for such work ranged from a mere 5s. to 6s.6d. for main line passenger drivers, the men at the top of their class. At that time platelayers got 18s. a week, porters 17s. John's father had £1 as an examiner. An ordinary fireman earned 19s. a week, increasing to 24s. for an express passenger fireman.

Even when the working shift was twelve hours it was not unusual for John and other drivers to work a fifteen hour day. He could recall having worked a ninety hour week on a Kelty job.

Those were boom times in the Central Fife coalfield. Its numerous collieries were linked to the ports, and particularly Methil, by a network of railway lines. There were branches to Kelty, to Lochore, to Lumphinans. From Townhill, Dunfermline, there were lines to Whitemyre, Drumtuthill and Wallsend collieries. At Oakley, there were branches to Kineddar and the Saline Valley collieries.

At the start of a shift a driver was given a handwritten list of orders for the day. This usually consisted of taking loaded wagons of coal to Methil or Burntisland, then taking back a full load of empties to the various collieries served by these ports. This often meant a fifteen or sixteen hour spell of duty.

Bad weather, such as foggy, rainy or stormy nights, could make the drivers task a fearsome one. Railways at that time were poorly lit, whilst the colliery sidings had no artificial lighting at all. The driver had a paraffin torch, his guard a handlamp, and with this inadequate illumination they had to reconnoitre the traffic in the sidings to assess how best shunting operations should be carried out.

In bad weather this was a miserable as well as a difficult job, even though the colliery staff could usually be relied upon to do everything possible to assist.

At that period, too, the Fife pits were doing a big bunker trade, with the many ships using Glasgow docks. Almost every night, ten or twelve trains would leave Fife with coal for Glasgow. The engines on these trains were small Wheatleys or Drummonds and their allotment was 20–24 wagons of eight tons capacity. The men used to book off at Glasgow and sleep at Cowlairs in the brake van. Driver and guard slept on the wooden tool boxes which lined either side of the van, while the fireman would put a plank across the passageway between the boxes at the back and sleep on that. Not only had they to put up with the discomfort of a hard surface but they were also likely to have a very rude awakening should their van be involved in shunting operations. It was not unknown for them to be shot from 'bed' onto the floor of the van.

Train crews in those days took a 'piece' with them in a tin box, the 'piece' usually consisting of bread and cheese, or eggs, or kippers. In the 'good old days', when crews booked off at Cowlairs they would go to a nearby restaurant which catered for railwaymen, for a cheap meal and a stone greybeard filled with tea. Later still the company also provided rest houses at important termini, where booked-off crews could

J38 No.65909 at Thornton beneath the massive coaling plant. This engine is seen here after transfer from St. Margarets and before our 62A depot plate was affixed to the smokebox. The J38 was designed by Sir Nigel Gresley for work in the Fife area and was a predecessor to his J39s.
[W. Laird]

sleep in comfort.

On these turns, until the advent of superheated locomotives, it was not unusual for a fireman to shovel eight or nine tons of coal in the course of a shift. Saturated steam engines were, of course, very wasteful and sheer drudgery for the fireman. At the start of the 262-mile run from Edinburgh to Aberdeen and back, the tender of such a locomotive was dangerously overloaded. The unfortunate fireman might shovel up to ten tons of coal into the firebox in the course of the journey. A superheater doubled the temperature of the steam, 'dried' it, and cut the engine's coal consumption by half.

Although Fife was long thought of as a museum where ancient locomotives could be seen in action, it is a remarkable and commendable fact that accidents of any kind were few despite how busy its lines were. Only one major accident is recorded in its railway history. This incident, known as the 'Burntisland Disaster', occurred in the early morning of 14 April 1914.

To quote from the Dunfermline press: "An appalling accident occurred on the main line of the North British Railway early on Tuesday morning, the London to Aberdeen express colliding just outside Burntisland station with the engine of a goods train which was being shunted to a siding." In fact this was being shunted on to the up line to allow a clear passage for the express which was headed by Atlantic No.872, *Auld Reekie.*

This was thrown off the rails by the impact and rolled down the short embankment on to the Burntisland links, where it embedded itself in the sand. Dragged with it were four coaches, only one of which, fortunately, carried passengers. The loss of life and injury was marvellously small compared to the extent of the smash. The driver, John Dickson of Aberdeen, and the fireman, William MacDonald of Arbroath, were buried under the tender and killed, and thirteen passengers were injured more or less seriously.

A Carlisle-Dundee goods was the other train involved. This was running in front of the express and was being shunted to clear the down line. All but the engine was clear when the express came thundering along and struck the goods engine (No.367) a glancing blow.

The N.B. Atlantics, one of which was involved in this Burntisland accident, were eventually replaced by Gresley Pacifics but their introduction was not a straightforward business. The Chief Civil Engineer for Scotland would not permit these giants to use the Forth Bridge until a test had been carried out. So, a Sunday was set aside for this purpose and locomotive Inspector John Allan, along with the Bridge Engineer William Russell (later District Engineer at Thornton), sent two Pacifics on to the bridge to stand on the central tower, while another Pacific on the other line raced past at the maximum bridge speed of 40m.p.h. This test was repeated on one of the connecting viaducts between the north and central towers. A Pacific, fully loaded with coal and water, weighed some 150 tons.

As signals to the engineer's staff under the bridge, the moving Pacific passed over and exploded detonators at the start and finish of the section under test. No deflection was recorded by their instruments during either test, which showed that the strength of the bridge was greater than anyone had realised.

The locomotives taking part in these tests were *William Whitelaw* (No.60004), *Hyperion* (No.60037) and *Sir Visto* (No.60068).

For close on half a century the Forth Bridge remained the most massive and daring bridge in the world. Yet, in its long history it has been happily free of accidents. Only one derailment has ever taken place on it, an incident that occurred during World War Two when a train from Perth was derailed as the result of a piece of iron falling from a goods train. No one was injured but the passenger train was held up for three hours. The passenger engine as a point of interest was *Bantam Cock* (No.3401, later B.R. No.61700) which, along with No.3402 (B.R. 1701), was built as an experiment. Although unnamed, the latter was affectionately known as 'Bantam Hen'. The driver of the derailed train was James Swan of Haymarket, the same driver who had been involved in the Haymarket Tunnel smash in 1932. It is said his hair went white after the Tunnel accident; I can vouch for it being whiter than white when I first knew him in 1935.

It's all history now, but a seven-mile stretch of line between Bridge of Earn and Glenfarg with a rising gradient of 1 in 75 was for many years used as the testing ground for the hauling power of locomotives operating on the Scottish East Coast line. The ability of a locomotive to haul its load up the steepest gradient on a given route is the deciding factor in the running time of certain train journeys. Further, the lighter the load on the 'up' gradient, the shorter the given running time.

Famous trials included those of 1917, 1921 and 1923. The first mentioned were on a stretch of line through the Ochils to Glenfarg with the North Eastern's two-cylinder 2–8–0 class, the North British directors being impressed by its performance.

The best known of the Ochils trials took place in 1921 when, under test, were the Great Western 2–8–0 No.2804; the North Eastern three-cylinder No.903; and Reid's No.8, with George Thornton at the throttle. Two years later North Eastern 0–8–0 No.2253 and Great Central 2–8–0 No.1185 performed trials for load and time on the Thornton Junction-Dundee run.

An outcome of these trials was an increase of the load for a Reid 0–6–0 from 27 wagons of coal to 30, each of these being of 12 tons weight and over. The experiment with the Great Central engine resulted in an increase in the standard load for the Townhill Junction to Aberdeen journey to 40 12-ton wagons hauled by Holmes 0–6–0 or to 30 by Reid's 0–6–0. The L.N.E.R. sent 20 of the 2–8–0 class to the sheds of Dunfermline, Thornton Junction, Dundee and Aberdeen. These engines were stored at Ormskirk after the 1914-18 war and were sold by the War Department to the L.N.E.R.

On the passenger trains, loads increased fantastically – from 100 tons up to no less than 500 tons for the Glen, Scott, Director, Shire and Pacifics. It was common practice during World War Two for Gresley Pacifics to pull out of the Waverley on the run to Kings Cross with 20 coaches of around 600 tons gross! On such occasions a pilot engine, pushing from behind, would assist the Pacific to work this load over the Dunbar-Granthouse stretch. A pilot at Newcastle and York would also assist to start the train out of the station, but otherwise leave the Pacific to manage to Kings Cross.

With the increase in power went an increase in engine and tender length overall, so new turntables had to be provided at certain points to deal with the new large locomotives. At Dunfermline, for example, a turntable of 50′ diameter and vacuum power-operated was installed in the area behind Piggies Lane.

Growing traffic had made necessary more powerful locomotives; hand-in-hand with this went the increase in size of wagons and increases in the dimensions and comfort of passenger coaches. While the standard full weight of the latter in the early days was 15 or 20 tons, and that of freight wagons about 8 tons, these increased over the years to coaches of 50 tons and wagons of 12–16 tons. A passenger train load in the early days might run from 60 to 80 tons; with the advent of the Pacifics ten coach-loads of 500 tons became the norm.

With the increase in the number and size of locomotives, coaling became a growing problem. This was solved by mechanisation, but the change from coaling by hand to mechanical coaling caused something near public uproar in Dunfermline. The noise of the mechanical coaler at work brought complaints, in particular from the Northern Hospital, which lay in close proximity. This was minimised as much as possible, and as an additional measure the whistling of locomotives during the night was prohibited – the railway authorities decreeing that telephone communication between the shed exit and the signalbox at Touch North should be substituted for whistle signals.

During my time at Thornton, John (Jock) Swanson was a young driver, and deputy foreman when the need arose. With all this combined effort for British Railways he was, understandably, a tired man and often overslept. An alarm clock was useless on these occasions and Jock would sleep on in blissful ignorance of his indispensability to British Railways. When I was foreman on the shift I knew only too well that his non-appearance at the booked time was his inability to distinguish between normal sleep and hibernation. However, his adaptability while at work and his knowledgeable keenness were assets to be appreciated, so I used to send a wakener to the nearby village to rouse this dormant driver. Once out of bed Jock was on the job in a matter of minutes. This was a long time ago and now Jock Swanson has become a respected driver at York. There, he failed to reach the eyesight standard for main line driving and was obliged to wear glasses. He could still see the funny side of this. He joked about his 'white stick' and how its use made a clearance for him on a crowded platform as he felt his way to the driving cab. He said that if he acquired a 'guide dog' and an inspector objected to the dog's presence in the driving cab he would say, "What's wrong with you? The dog's not driving!"

In his steam days at Thornton, he remembers a driver called Tom Aitken who was on a Glasgow passenger train one day. His fireman was Jock Cummings and Tom's idea of a good fireman was 'head down and a— up'. He and Jock didn't get on very well together. On this particular occasion he was at the end of his tether and said to Jock, "I am asking for another fireman at Glesca". Jock's incredible bulk oozed sweat and his round, red face glistened in the fireglow as he laboured to maintain steam. "Thank God for that," he answered, "I could do with a hand!" . . .

Jock Swanson fired to 'Pout' Henderson for a time and remembers returning from Edinburgh with a B1 on a freight destined for Thornton. On reaching Kirkcaldy the tender was absolutely cleared of coal and to enable them to finish the journey they 'borrowed' some from a wagon in Kirkcaldy yard. The coal merchants name on the wagon was Reekie and as Jock says, 'What a funny name for a coal man!'

Driver Tom Blackwood was on the same job the following week and like many more enginemen, he was keen on overtime to increase his earnings. One particular morning Tom was running early and as he was filling the locomotive tank at Niddrie West he wondered how he was going to delay his return to Thornton. Just then his mate decided to trim the coal and a huge lump fell off the tender, hitting Tom on the head. He ended up on overtime at Edinburgh Royal Infirmary but, after a doctor had stitched his head, the request was for an ambulance to take him to Niddrie so that he could work his train back to Thornton!

Tom was so thin – probably with working so much overtime – that, when he went to Burntisland Bathing Pool, the rubber ring supplied to hold the locker key kept falling off his wrist, so he had to put it on his ankle.

Looking back on my life as a locomotive-man I sometimes wonder if I chose the right profession. Years of shift work seems to have deprived me of so much. At the time I was too engrossed in earning a living and did not realise myself and my family were often in different worlds. Normal social activity was impossible and when I was free in the evening I had to think about an early rise next morning. Most of the time there were seven working days (or nights) in a week and the recreation taken for granted by most people was a rare event to me. When I felt like improving my education at evening classes these, too, were out of the question and I had to settle for lessons by correspondence. There were compensations for some shift workers, such as those who had the energy to play a round of golf or go swimming after working night shift or early day shift. Nowadays, the deprivation we readily accepted goes under the name of 'unsocial hours' and warrants extra payment. But, what you never have, you never miss . . . I feel I have been adequately rewarded for any sacrifices on my part because throughout my working life I knew contentment and that is something of rare value. The satisfaction I experienced was founded on hard work and the incessant demands of the steam engine. There are now, and will be in the future, more wonderful inventions but I doubt if there will ever be a working relationship to compare with the steam engineman and his engine, or a more fascinating machine for man to wed.

books from

D. BRADFORD BARTON LTD

Great Western Steam in Action edited by L.M. Collins
Great Western Steam in Action: 2 edited by L.M. Collins
Great Western Steam in Action: 3 edited by L.M. Collins
Great Western Steam in Action: 4 edited by L.M. Collins
Great Western Steam in Action: 5 edited by L.M. Collins
Great Western Steam in Action: 6 edited by L.M. Collins
Great Western Steam in Action: 7 edited by L.M. Collins
Great Western Steam through the Years: 1 Tony Fairclough & Alan Wills
Great Western Steam through the Years: 2 Tony Fairclough & Alan Wills
Great Western Branch Line Steam: 1 edited by C.L. Williams
Great Western Branch Line Steam: 2 edited by C.L. Williams
Great Western Steam Miscellany: 1 edited by C.L. Williams
Great Western Steam Miscellany: 2 edited by C.L. Williams
Great Western Steam in the West Country edited by '4588'
Great Western Steam on Shed edited by C.L. Williams
More Great Western Steam on Shed edited by C.L. Williams
Great Western Steam in Close Up edited by P.W.B. Semmens
Great Western Steam at Swindon Works Brian Morrison
Great Western Steam Preserved edited by Grenville R. Hounsell
Great Western Steam South of the Severn R.E. Toop
Great Western Steam in Cornwall B.A. Butt & Tony Fairclough
More Great Western Steam in Cornwall Tony Fairclough
Great Western Steam in Devon edited by Tony Fairclough
More Great Western Steam in Devon Tony Fairclough & Alan Wills
Great Western Steam off the Beaten Track G.F. Bannister
Great Western Steam in South Wales S. Rickard
More Great Western Steam in South Wales S. Rickard
Great Western Steam in the Midlands Michael Mensing
Great Western Steam Doubleheaded edited by C.L. Williams
More Great Western Steam Doubleheaded edited by do.
Great Western Steam in Wales & the Border Counties edited by C.L. Williams
More Great Western Steam in Wales & the Border Counties edited by C.L. Williams
Great Western Steam through the Cotswolds C.L. Williams
Great Western Steam around Bristol edited by C.L. Williams
The last decade of Great Western Main Line Steam T.E. Williams
GWR Service Timetable Appendices 1945

London Midland Steam in Action edited by W. Askew Blake
London Midland Steam in Action: 2 edited by W. Askew Blake
London Midland Steam in Action: 3 edited by W. Askew Blake
London Midland Steam in Action: 4 edited by W. Askew Blake
London Midland Steam Locomotives: 1 Brian Morrison
London Midland Steam Locomotives: 2 Brian Morrison
London Midland Steam from Lineside Brian Morrison
London Midland Steam in the Midlands Michael Mensing
London Midland Steam Over Shap Derek Cross
London Midland Steam in the Northern Fells Derek Cross
London Midland Steam North of the Border Derek Cross
London Midland Steam in North Wales W.G. Rear
London Midland Steam Doubleheaded edited by W. Askew Blake
London Midland Steam in the East Midlands J.F. Henton
London Midland Steam on the ex-L&Y edited by R.S. Greenwood
London Midland Steam on Shed compiled by '45562'
London Midland Steam: Skipton to Carlisle R.H. Leslie

London Midland Steam in Yorkshire P. Cookson
London Midland Steam in the North West J.R. Carter
More London Midland Steam in the North West N. Dyckhoff
London Midland Steam in the Peak District J.R. Hillier
London Midland Steam around Carlisle R.H. Leslie
LMSR Steam 1923-1948 H.C. Casserley
LMSR Locomotives 1923-1948: 1 H.C. Casserley
LMSR Locomotives 1923-1948: 2 H.C. Casserley
LMSR Locomotives 1923-1948: 3 H.C. Casserley
(de-luxe available of above 4 vols)
LNWR Locomotives of C.J. Bowen Cooke O.S. Nock
Class 8F Stanier 2-8-0s Stanier 8F Loco Society

Southern Steam in Action: 1 Tony Fairclough & Alan Wills
Southern Steam in Action: 2 Tony Fairclough & Alan Wills
Southern Steam in Action: 3 Tony Fairclough & Alan Wills
Southern Steam in Action: 4 Tony Fairclough & Alan Wills
Southern Steam 1923-1939 John L. Smith
Southern Steam from Lineside Derek Cross
Southern Steam South and East Stanley Creer
More Southern Steam South and East Stanley Creer
Southern Steam South and West Tony Fairclough & Alan Wills
More Southern Steam South and West Tony Fairclough & Alan Wills
Southern Steam on the Isle of Wight Tony Fairclough & Alan Wills
Southern Steam on Shed Tony Fairclough & Alan Wills
More Southern Steam on Shed Tony Fairclough & Alan Wills
Southern Steam Locomotive Survey:
1: **early Maunsell classes** Tony Fairclough & Alan Wills
2: **later Maunsell classes** Tony Fairclough & Alan Wills
3: **Merchant Navy Pacifics** Tony Fairclough & Alan Wills
4: **Bulleid Light Pacifics** Tony Fairclough & Alan Wills
5: **Urie classes** Tony Fairclough & Alan Wills
6: **Drummond classes** Tony Fairclough & Alan Wills
7: **Adams classes** Tony Fairclough & Alan Wills
8: **Wainwright classes** Tony Fairclough & Alan Wills
Southern Steam Doubleheaded Tony Fairclough & Alan Wills
Southern Steam in the West Country Tony Fairclough & Alan Wills
More Southern Steam in the West Country Tony Fairclough & Alan Wills
Southern Electrics edited by B.W. Rayner
Southern Branch Line Steam: 1 Tony Fairclough & Alan Wills
Southern Branch Line Steam: 2 Tony Fairclough & Alan Wills
Southern Steam through the Years Tony Fairclough & Alan Wills
Steam on the Brighton Line edited by A.C. Perryman
Recollections of the Southern Between the Wars H.C. Casserley
Bodmin & Wadebridge Railway Tony Fairclough & Alan Wills
Southern Steam in Works Tony Fairclough & Alan Wills
Southern Steam in Close Up Tony Fairclough & Alan Wills
SR Working Timetable Appendices 1934

North Eastern Steam in Action Brian Morrison
North Eastern Steam from Lineside P.J. Lynch
North Eastern Steam in Northumbria Malcolm Dunnett
North Eastern Pacifics Norman E. Preedy
North Eastern Steam Locomotive Album P.J. Lynch
LNER Locomotives 1923-1948 H.C. Casserley
LNER Steam 1923-1948 H.C. Casserley

BR Diesels in Action edited by G. Weekes
BR Diesels in Action: 2 edited by G. Weekes
BR Diesels in Action: 3 edited by G. Weekes
BR Diesels in Action: 4 edited by G. Weekes

BR Diesels in Action: 5 edited by G. Weekes
BR Diesels on Shed N.E. Preedy
BR Diesels in Close-Up N.E. Preedy & H.L. Ford
BR Diesels in the Landscape Derek Cross
WR Diesel-Hydraulics Norman E. Preedy & G.F. Gillham
BR Diesels and Electrics around Britain A.W. Hobson
BR Diesels Doubleheaded edited by G. Weekes
Diesels in London and the Home Counties P.A. Dobson
Diesels on Eastern Region edited by Norman E. Preedy
Diesels on Western Region edited by H.L. Ford
Diesels on Scottish Region S. Rickard
Diesels on Midland Region edited by G. Weekes
Diesels in the Highlands edited by G. Weekes
Diesels in the West Midlands and Central Wales G.F. Bannister
Diesels on Cornwall's Main Line H.L. Ford
Diesels on the Devon Main Line edited by H.L. Ford
Modern Rail Album A.W. Hobson
Branch Lines Round Britain in the Diesel Era J.A.M. Vaughan
DMUs Countrywide P.J. Fowler
The Westerns: BR Class 52 Diesel-Hydraulics H.L. Ford
The Warships: BR Class 42/43 Diesel-Hydraulics H.L. Ford
BR Diesel Miscellany: 1 edited by G. Weekes
BR Diesels in Detail M. Oakley & Brian Morrison
Diesels West G.F. Gillham

BR Standard Steam in Action Derek Cross
BR Standard 2-10-0 Class 9F edited by G. Weekes
BR Standard Steam in Close-Up Tony Fairclough & Alan Wills
BR Standard Britannia Pacifics edited by G. Weekes
Memories of Steam around Britain P.J. Lynch
Scottish Steam in the 1920s R.D. Stephen
Scottish Steam Miscellany R.D. Stephen
Scottish Branch Line Steam edited by Jack Kernahan
Scottish Main Line Steam edited by Jack Kernahan
Steam in the Western Highlands edited by Jack Kernahan
Last Decade of Scottish Steam Derek Cross
Steam on the Waverley Route R.H. Leslie
Steam on Britain's Miniature Railways Robin Butterell
Steam on the Somerset & Dorset G.A. Richardson
Steam around Britain in the Seventies L.A. Nixon
Cornwall's Railways A. Fairclough
The Railways of Devon A. Kingdom
Specials in Action A.R. Butcher
Mineral Railways of the West Country Tony Fairclough
Industrial Steam Adrian J. Booth
British Steam around the Regions K.R. Pirt & D.E. Penney
The Tralee & Dingle Railway David G. Rowlands
European Narrow Gauge Steam: 1 D. Trevor Rowe
European Narrow Gauge Steam: 2 D. Trevor Rowe
Industrial Narrow Gauge Railways in Britain P.D. Nicholson
British Narrow Gauge Steam edited by Michael J. Messenger
More British Narrow Gauge Steam Michael J. Messenger
Steam on the SNCF Peter F. Winding
European Steam in Action P.J. Lynch
Austrian Steam from Lineside V.C.K. Allen
Portuguese Steam from Lineside V.C.K. Allen
Railways of the Republic of Ireland 1925-1975 M.H.C. Baker
Articulated Locomotives of the World Donald Binns
South American Steam M.H.J. Finch
Steam in India Hugh Hughes
Steam in the Andes Brian Fawcett
New Zealand Steam Spectacular Derek Cross
British-Built Steam Locomotives Overseas J.N. Westwood
Vulcan Foundry Locomotives 1832-1956 D.E. Gudgin
Electric Locomotives of the World F.J.G. Haut

Steam Super-Power around the World R.K. Evans
Light Railways around Britain H.C. Casserley
The later years of Metropolitan Steam H.C. Casserley
Irish Railways in the Heyday of Steam H.C. Casserley
The Midland Railway edited by The Midland Railway Trust
Steam in Australia C.B. Gilbertson
The Great Central Recalled George Dow
North British Steam Locomotives Overseas John H. Court
North British Steam Locomotives in Britain John H. Court
On the Welsh Narrow Gauge J.I.C. Boyd
Scottish Railways in the Heyday of Steam H.C. Casserley
European Trams L.F. Folkard
British Trams L.F. Folkard
Lynton and Barnstaple Railway J.R. Yeomans
Border Steam Peter Brock
Diesel Super-Power around the World R.K. Evans
Welsh Railways in the Heyday of Steam H.C. Casserley
On the Isle of Man Narrow Gauge J.I.C. Boyd

Paperbacks etc

BR Standard Freight Wagons D. Larkin
Private Owner Freight Wagons D. Larkin
Pre-Nationalisation Freight Wagons D. Larkin
BR General Parcels Rolling Stock D. Larkin
BR Departmental Rolling Stock D. Larkin

Class 44/46 Diesels (The Peaks) J.A. Walker
Brush-Sulzer Class 47 Diesel-electrics edited by B. Ringer
Electrics of West Coast Main Line Roly Longhurst
EE Class 50 Diesel-electrics Michael Oakley
BR-EE Class 37 Diesel-electrics D & E.G.
BR Diesel Shunting Locos D. & E.G.
BR Diesels Departed Derek Cross
BR Diesel Cavalcade Brian Morrison
BR Diesel Freight (Traditional Era) Michael Oakley
BR Diesel Freight (Era of Specialisation) Michael Oakley
Industrial Diesels—a pictorial survey A.J. Booth

LNER Footplate Memories Charles Meacher
When there was Steam—memories of a fireman Tony Barfield
On the Footplate—memories of a GWR Engineman J. Drayton
A Loco Fireman Looks Back: WR Recollections
Ray Gwillam
Steam Supreme—recollections of Scottish Railways in the 1920s,
R.D. Stephen
Drawn by Steam—memories of a Tyseley locoman L.C. Jacks
Firing Days at Saltley T.R. Essery
Locomotives at War—Army railway reminiscences of the Second World War P.M. Kalla-Bishop

Vale of Rheidol Pictorial J. Reeves
Welshpool & Llanfair Railway Pictorial Ralph Cartwright
The Cornwall Railway R.J. Woodfin
Spirit of Steam Roy Sinclair (New Zealand)
The London RT Bus P.J. Lynch
Redruth and Chasewater Railway D.B. Barton
Southern Locomotives to Scale Ian Beattie
LMSR Locomotives to Scale Ian Beattie